1985

MAKING MORAL DECISIONS

Making Moral Decisions

Edward Stevens

PAULIST PRESS
New York/Ramsey

Nihil Obstat:
Reverend George M. Keating
Censor Librorum

Imprimatur:
+ Most Reverend Peter L. Gerety, D. D.
Archbishop of Newark

July 8, 1981

Contents

Foreword

Every day swirling moral controversies confront us on the television screen, in the newspaper, and on the political and legal scene. There is no place to hide. People have asked me where they might find out in capsule form what the fight is all about, the issues for and against. This book is an attempt to answer that need, a need so strong that I believe it justifies the dangers inherent in covering so many complex questions in such a relatively small space. I intend to stimulate thought, to get the debate going, but not to write the full discussion, and certainly not to settle it.

Concrete moral issues are defined by facts, experience and the disciplined use of reason. Hence my approach is philosophical, not theological. Religion will color the way in which the issues are seen. Protestant, Jew, Catholic, Buddhist and humanist will each view the issues through colored glasses of slightly different tints; values will be stressed somewhat differently in terms of different religious orientations and goals. But a common humanity unites them all. Therefore I have tried to line up the issues in terms of the human use of reason. I leave it to the reader to view these issues through his or her own religious spectacles and to correct whatever bias might be introduced by those of the author.

Preface

For many people morality is a dead issue. Strident voices are raised for and against war, for and against premarital sex, for and against drug use, for and against open housing. There are plenty of strong feelings, plenty of easily made charges of "hypocrite" or "corrupt," but no solid moral grounds on which one can stand secure. Law, order, morality and religion seem to have caved in. In the midst of this moral chaos, where can we take our stand? Is morality a hopelessly dead issue in this complex and changing world?

This is not a religion book. Religion doesn't have the answer to moral questions. Nor is this an answer book, for there are no absolute answers. This is a book on morality. And that fact may cause many to ask: "Why not religion? Why no absolute answers?"

In the past, religion had been able to serve both as the determiner and the guardian of morals, and in more primitive tight-knit societies it still serves this function. A religion-based morality can be extremely useful for the stability of a society. When a certain society depends upon institutions like slavery or property rights or kingly authority, for example, then it is extremely advantageous to give these institutions a divine sanction. People have used religion to present their own social norms as established by God, and hence as universally and absolutely valid and disobeyed only at the risk of divine punishment. This works well as long as no one is aware that other societies are proclaiming completely contradictory norms as universally and absolutely valid manifestations of God's will. Therefore, we can have, for example, the strange sight of opposing armies enthusiastically charging into battle, both sides doing their slaughtering "for God."

This is not the place to examine the role of religion in today's world. However, one thing is clear. Whatever religion can do, it cannot supply moral answers in today's pluralistic world. When religion takes over the realm of morality, it takes humanly made institutions and declares them to be sacred norms. We thus end up with as many moral codes as there are societies and as there are religions in societies. Even a religion like Roman Christianity, which in the past has claimed to have access to specially revealed moral truths, is getting very few definite answers from that source today.

The fact is that human beings make moral norms. Religion can preach them, claim that they are the divine will and promise rewards and punishments, but moral codes are human constructions. All we have to go on are our minds, our hearts and each other. Humans are intelligent; humans are free; humans are social. This is the basis of morality upon which this book builds, and such a basis—intelligence, freedom and love or sociality—is inherently sound.

Are there absolute *answers* to moral problems? No. Problems and situations change continually. Different problems have different answers, as first-grade arithmetic makes clear. Are there absolute *values?* Yes. Intelligence is an absolute good. Stupidity, even in the name of religion, is not to be preferred to intelligence. I cannot prove that intelligence is better than stupidity. I simply choose values, live them, and they prove themselves. If you proclaim stupidity in the name of Communism or Mohammedanism or Americanism as a value to be preferred to intelligence, we have reached the parting of the ways regarding the argument of this book. Similarly, this book supposes that love is a value to be chosen over hate, and freedom over nonfreedom. Later, these values will be further explored.

Therefore, although there are no absolute *answers* to moral problems, there are absolute *values.* There are also absolute *principles.* A principle is not an answer. A principle is that which can lead to an answer. "A stitch in time saves nine" is a principle. This principle can lead me to conclude that the loose button on my overcoat should be made secure. The principle may be absolute, but that does not mean that the conclusion should also be made into an absolute. Though it may always be true that "a stitch in time saves nine," I cannot therefore conclude that "loose buttons should always be secured." Perhaps I should replace the loose buttons with a zipper, or throw the coat away.

In this book, the absolute values of intelligence, freedom and sociality will be the basis of absolute moral principles. When faced with a moral problem, I will ask three questions: "What is the intelligent thing to do?" (Intelligence here is serving as a principle.) "What solution will foster the freedom of the individuals involved?" (Freedom here is serving as a principle.) "What solution will best promote the common good?" (Sociality here is serving as a moral principle.) Again, a moral principle is not an answer, although it can lead to an answer to a moral problem. And an absolute moral principle need not lead to an absolute moral answer. It has wisely been said that one person's answers serve as the basis for another person's questions.

Why do I choose intelligence, freedom and sociality as absolute values and as the basis for absolute moral principles? The basic principle behind my choice is: "Nature is the measure of action." The moral person does not deny his nature, whereas immoral persons are self-destructive. They are unfaithful to what it means to be human. To be human is to be intelligent, to be free and to be social. Hence intelligence, freedom and sociality have been chosen as basic human values and as principles of morality. Human nature is the measure of action. Behind every philosophy of morals lies a philosophy of humankind. The philosophy in this book is that humans are intelligent, free and social. Hence ethical solutions which foster stupidity, non-freedom and hatred are immoral.

There are other philosophies with different basic values, and hence different moral principles and different ethical conclusions. The primacy of scientific intelligence would not be a basic value in a Bantu philosophy or a moral principle in Bantu ethics. How do I know that my values and principles are better than Bantu values and principles? Values cannot be logically proved, but only chosen and lived, and in this way they will prove (or disprove) themselves. The best this book can do is invite the reader to consider an ethics based on intelligence, freedom and sociality. If you choose such an ethics, where will it lead? Will it prove or disprove itself?

4

Part I explores these basic human values more deeply. There we will consider the meaning, limits and implications of intelligence, freedom and sociality. In other words, we will outline our philosophy and indicate how it will be the basis for our approach to all the complex problems considered in the remainder of the book. In the following sections we will consider particular moral problems which have arisen in contemporary American society.

For reasons which should now be clear, our approach will be heuristic rather than dogmatic, experimental rather than *a priori*. We will try to steer a middle course between a moral dogmatism dispensing absolute solutions and a moral skepticism which despairs of obtaining any answers at all. Each particular topic will be treated in four steps. First, we will try to clarify a particular problem that is causing moral concern. Then we will present the arguments for and against the morality of the particular behavior in question. Immediately thereafter, we will sum up the issues which should be considered in coming to a moral conclusion. Finally, the author will venture some observations of his own on the problem at issue. Each chapter will end with a few suggestions for further readings on the topics treated.

Therefore the main purpose of the book is not to give the author's conclusions but to assist the readers in coming to their own conclusions. The author's bias may sometimes be evident in the particular treatments, although an effort was made to treat both sides of every question in an objective and balanced way. The author has already admitted a bias toward a philosophy in which freedom, intelligence and sociality are central values.

This book does not deny a religious dimension to life any more than it denies an artistic dimension. It does deny that either particular religions or particular works of art are competent of themselves to furnish answers to the concrete moral conflicts which arise in human living. After all, Christ himself passed *moral* judgment on the *religion* of his day, as did Gautama Buddha in his. Just how the religious and aesthetic dimensions of experience positively enrich human life must be the subject matter of another kind of study than this book purports to be.

*   *   *

This new edition has been revised from cover to cover. First, as to the form, anachronisms are deleted. And the language has been brought into line with the sexual and racial sensibilities of the eighties.

As for content, a treatment of the new reproductive technologies replaces the issue of heart transplants in the original edition. Part V has been expanded to deal with Social Justice from a feminist perspective, and to examine our obligations to less developed Third World nations. Finally, the bibliographical suggestions at the end of each question have been completely updated.

February 1981

PART I
Morality and Human Nature

INTRODUCTION. Consider first what the word *moral* means. We read of men and women being picked up on "morals" charges, but morality governs more than sexual behavior. We read the works of anthropologists on the *mores* or customs of a society. But this is too wide a meaning. The fact that most Americans have the custom of eating mashed potatoes with a fork is not necessarily a moral issue. Morality is concerned with those actions which make someone a good human being or a bad human being. I can be a star salesperson and a bad human being. Or I can be a bad professional quarterback and go home to hear my wife tell me: "That's all right, honey; you're a good man." Morality looks at one not as a salesperson or a quarterback or a student or a judge, but as a human being, with everything that this means. Actions which are consistent with what it means to be a fully human person are morally good. Actions which are unfaithful to what it means to be a fully human person are morally evil.

All right, you say, but how do I know what it means to be a fully human person? Yes, there's the catch. That's why we can have arguments about morality. You may have one idea of what it means to be human, while I may have another. In other words, we may have different philosophies of human nature. We presuppose in this book a philosophy centered around the human values of intelligence, freedom and sociality. Let's explore the meaning of each of these terms a little more deeply.

1.

Do you *teach* people to be moral or do you *train* them? Does the experience of moral obligation demand that a person be intelligent about his or her behavior?

THE PROBLEM. The fat lady says: "I know I shouldn't eat this strawberry shortcake, but it is too good to resist." I can *know* what is good, but not do it. On the other hand, a child can be brought up to be a "good little boy," but be completely unable to give you the reasons why he is a good little boy. Morality seems to be a matter of good training, not good education. If this is true, then the present book is a rather fatuous enterprise, for it assumes that a person should be intelligent about behavior, that it is worthwhile to give the reasons for and against affirmative action, cocaine-use or abortion. But if morality is a matter of attitudes rather than beliefs, of emotions rather than rationally held convictions, of training rather than education, then it is of little import for morality whether or not man is rational and reflective. What we need are training schools for humans, much as we have training schools for dogs. And such schools do indeed exist.

ARGUMENTS FOR AND AGAINST. What right do I have to classify intelligence as a human value essential to morality? Well, there is no question that dogs and children and even soldiers and others can be trained to blindly perform tricks and actions of various kinds. But when a person acts blindly, we say that he isn't responsible for what he's doing. When a dog wins a blue ribbon at the dog show, it's the owner and trainer we are rewarding, not the dog. I don't feel responsible for the things I do blindly. I would feel hurt if I were punished, and guilty or at least surprised if I were rewarded, for something I didn't know I was doing. That's why I resent being fined for unconsciously speeding in a speed trap.

The superego could be called *unconscious* conscience. Early parental training implants moral taboos in us which become part of our *automatic* behavior. Most of us are "well trained" in many ways. But superego is not rationally *reflective* conscience. Moral responsibility implies reflective action, "knowing what you're doing." It's this area of reflective activity which concerns a book on morality. Moral responsibility is a function of conscious reflective behavior, not of blind conformity. I simply do not hold myself or others responsible for actions done blindly.

Therefore, superego is not moral conscience. Superego refers to the automatic taboos and guilt feelings implanted by early training. Conscience concerns my reflective conscious choices made possible by moral education rather than by blind training. Both dimensions are involved in most of our moral activity. The blind and unconscious are intermingled with the reflective and conscious. Moral maturity comes about as we move more and more of our behavior from the unconscious to the conscious and reflective level. The morally mature man refrains from adultery not because of blind guilt feelings but rather because of a consciously chosen and nurtured respect and love for his wife.

As you read the succeeding chapters of this book, you may often get the urge to object that people just aren't that rational, that they often are blindly agressive and selfish, inhibited by sexual taboos and driven by blind prejudices, that you can't reason with children but have to punish them, and that even adults are more moved by blind fear than by sweet reason in their moral lives. When you object in this way, you are absolutely right. Behavior does have its blind, irrational, unconscious side. Maybe ninety-five percent of it is such. The word "morality" is often applied to this behavior, and an entire book could be written on this subject. However, this book does not use the word "morality" in this way, nor does it intend to discuss explicitly the unconscious dimension of human behavior.

Our starting point is the experience of moral obligation. Moral obligation means that I feel responsible for my actions, and I feel responsible for my actions only to the extent that I know what I am doing. Morality in this book means only that behavior for which I feel responsible, insofar as I know what I am doing. Thus the appeal throughout the book is the appeal to intelligence. We are followers of Socrates and John Dewey inasmuch as we believe that "knowledge is virtue." Intelligence is a central value in the philosophy of man behind this moral approach. We are far from denying the irrational and animal side of human behavior. We just say that it does not pertain to responsible morality, that it diminishes responsibility, and that it is not relevant to the purpose of this book.

2.

Aren't we the victims of heredity, education, and environment, even though we don't realize it? Are we free enough for moral responsibility?

THE PROBLEM. Freedom is the opposite side of the coin of reflective intelligence. Because I can reflect on my actions and weigh alternatives against each other, I have the possibility for free action in a way that a rhinoceros or an alligator does not. In fact, many philosophers put freedom at the very heart and center of man's moral life. But on the other hand, it is argued that such apparent freedom is illusory. The alternative ways of acting really available to an individual are drastically narrowed or even disappear altogether when you consider the weight of all the forces pressing on and determining an individual's behavior.

ARGUMENTS FOR AND AGAINST. First, we are victims of our biology. A personality can be dramatically altered by a lobotomy, hormonal injections or truth drugs. This fact should help us to realize how very really, though less dramatically, we are determined in our actions by the state of our digestion or the tranquilizers we take. How much more pervasive, therefore, is the influence on a person of his inherited genetic structure and physiology! Consider the natural athlete, for example, whose exploits the less endowed may envy but cannot emulate.

Next, continues the determinist, there are the social pressures and determinants which make real freedom just an illusion. If you're born a Murphy, you act like a Murphy. Or if you are an American in a foreign land, people will point to you and say "There's an American" before you even open your mouth. Television, radio and the printed word affect our attitudes toward fashions, sex, wars, yardsticks of success, injustices, violence and patriotism in ways we usually don't begin to realize until we are uprooted and thrown into another culture which does not share these taken-for-granted values that we never before questioned. The deep affective need to conform in order to be secure makes it possible to automate, program and computerize human beings and even to predict their voting.

Thus we are the products of our social groups with their relentless propaganda, whether this fact results from sitting in front of a TV cartoon or on mother's knee. An Italian-American bank executive will never be mistaken for a Chinese coolie no matter how free he thinks he is. Moreover, we are the products of our inherited physiology and current biological health and condition. And worst of all, says the determinist, all of this is unconscious. Most people don't say, for example: "This is the American way of marriage," but rather: "This is *the* way marriage should be" (take the case of monogamy vs. polygamy). They don't say: "This is the American yardstick of success," but rather: "This is *the* way to recognize a successful man." And how many unconscious semi-neurotics among us relive over and over again their childhood battles and traumata without realizing it. Not only are we products and victims of our psychological, physiological and sociological pasts, but we are for the most part unconscious of this fact, and able to do little about even what we are conscious of.

There is more than a grain of truth in the determinist position. I have my own physiology and no one else's and it is going to determine to a great extent what I can and cannot do. I have my own psyche with its own scars, and it will shape my peculiar behavior patterns. In other words, I have a history. I live in a particular segment of space and time, with all the limitations this implies. I live in a particular body, with its limits shaped by particular societies and their peculiarities. I cannot pretend to be above history; moreover, I am not a disembodied spirit, nor do I exist in isolation from society. If to be free means to be above space, time, body and society, then I am not free. To the extent that my actions are determined in these ways, I am not morally responsible for them. I am what I am and can do nothing about it. I am only morally responsible to the extent that I am free. What does freedom mean for the historically conditioned man? A book on morality concerns the free behavior of man. It is up to psychology, sociology and physiology to explore the patterns of determination, the inevitable context of freedom.

Most people use these patterns of determination as excuses

to escape from the burden of freedom, according to Jean-Paul Sartre, philosopher of freedom *par excellence*. We do not dare to face the freedom that we really have. We would prefer to live in what he terms "bad faith." We prefer to pretend that "we can't help ourselves," that we have to follow the expectations of our family, the dictates of our Church, the laws of our country, the conventionalities of our jobs, the needlings of our friends. We'll look anywhere, blame anyone, rather than take upon ourselves the responsibility we have for our lives. The fact is—if we only had the courage to face it—that we are unbearably free, utterly alone in our decisions. For example, suppose that my religion forbids blood transfusions or birth control, and the health of my wife demands a blood transfusion or birth control. Where do I turn. "Tell me what to do!" I say to my pastor. "What do you want me to do?" I ask my wife. Which is better. a morality of personal love or a morality of religious obedience? No one can tell me. I am free and alone in my freedom. Most people cannot bear this and pretend that they are the victims of their Church or of their families. This is bad faith.

And so a soldier can burn down a civilian village. "Just obeying orders," he shrugs; "sorry about that." The hangman can drop the trap door with the thought: "It's all in a day's work." The social worker can cut off the welfare check from the mother who had one too many illegitimate children and tell her: "I'm sorry, but I'm just obeying the law." No one is responsible. It's "they," the "law," "God," "orders," "society"—anyone or anybody, apparently, except the people actually involved. This is bad faith—the refusal to be free.

The sociological phenomenon of "alternation" of roles bears out this freedom. It may be true that I am a Mohammedan. But there are many ways of playing the religion game besides the Mohammedan way. Why couldn't I change my religion game? Or suppose that I am an American. There are many ways of playing the patriotism game besides the American way. Ecuadorians are even more earnest and serious players—of the Ecuadorian game. Why not play Ecuadorian? The point is, Sartre might say, to play them freely. I am not a victim of society, though the coward in each of us would prefer to have it that way rather than face our responsibility. It's easier for the Nazi concentration camp guard to vaporize the inmates because he cannot "disobey orders" than to vaporize them freely and responsibly. It is bad faith to pretend he could not do otherwise. He could become an inmate himself, for example.

Therefore, we exist in history, in bodies and in societies. We are determined in many ways, for human freedom always exists in a context. Some of these determinations we cannot change—the law of gravity, for example, and many of our bodily and mental limitations. Many of them, expecially the social games, once we see them, we could change if we wished. It's easier to pretend to ourselves that we are victimized. Morality is not concerned with the determinations we cannot change any more than it is concerned with our blind unconscious behavior. You don't punish a paralytic child because he can't walk. It's not fair. He's not responsible. He cannot help it. The area of moral concern in this book and in our lives is human behavior that is reflective, conscious and free. This behavior will usually be bound up with much that is unconscious and unfree. It belongs to the sciences to investigate these determined patterns. But the moral question arises to the extent that our lives come under our conscious control. It is here that we are responsible. It is here that we can meaningfully ask the question: "What should I do in order to be a fully human person?" Morality demands a philosophy which recognizes the values of human intelligence and freedom.

3.

If we are free, are we social too? Is it bad faith to consider others in our moral decisions?

THE PROBLEM. The basic issue here is the relation of the individual and society. If the individual is free and alone in that freedom, it would seem that no one else can tell him what to do and decide his moral life for him. Yet the individual exists in society under laws, interacting with myriads of people who claim he has duties toward them. How far can and should the individual in the name of freedom stand up against family, country and Church? To be a fully human person, one must be intelligent and free. Is the individual also social? If so, how far? Here we have the whole gamut of opinions, from Thomas Hobbes who says that society is supreme, to Jean-Paul Sartre who says that the individual is supreme. Nature is the measure of action. Is society or the individual supreme? Or does the truth lie somewhere in between? Your answer to a whole range of moral questions from abortion to ecology will depend on your answer to this question.

THE ALTERNATIVES. We'll look first at the extreme positions of Thomas Hobbes and Jean-Paul Sartre, and then at the compromise positions suggested by the personalistic view in the so-called new morality and the evolutionary view of human nature in the philosophy of pragmatism. Which is the true story about the individual and society—"dog eat dog" or "no man is an island"?

To put it crudely, for both Sartre and Hobbes the human situation is best described as "dog eat dog." I *am* an island. I have no natural bonds uniting me to others. I am completely on my own, alone in my freedom, and so is everyone else. "Hell is other people," Sartre has said. Your freedom is a threat to mine. All personal meetings turn into a contest: Will I stare you down, have my way and maintain my integrity and freedom, or will you succeed in dominating me, making me fit into your world? As we have seen, most people in Sartre's view, live in bad faith. They let society browbeat them into submission. They give up their freedom to others under the pretext that they cannot help themselves: "I'm stuck; I have to obey the law (or God, or my friends, or the Church)."

The natural state of man, the way Hobbes puts it, is "the war of everybody against everybody else." If it were not for fear of the all-powerful arm of the law enforced by the State, you would attack me, rob me blind and do away with me if you could, since I am your natural enemy and would do the same to you if I had the chance. It is no accident that the greatest part of our taxes goes into national defense, police forces, riot squads, detective agencies and national and state guards. It is no accident that killing, rape and looting are rampant at times of national and civil disaster. The only things that stand between the precarious fabric of society and chaotic anarchy are the law and the fear of the power of the State.

Curiously, these two "dog eat dog" philosophies of human society come up with opposite views regarding individual freedom and the law. For Sartre, individual freedom is central, and I must maintain it at all costs against society which is always trying to take it away from me. Freedom is all I have. I make myself what I will be. Bad faith is the constant temptation to surrender to others my freedom, which is my very identity. I obey the law only if I freely choose to do so, only if the law represents the path of the kind of person I freely choose to be. Never would I obey the law against my will; never would I let society take over my life in a way that I do not freely choose. Civil disobedience, conscientious objection and revolution would find strong roots in this philosophy.

For Hobbes, on the other hand, law must be central. Law is the only thing which stands between society and chaos. Law is the only security I have against being put to death by other men who are my natural enemies. Never could I claim a moral right to disobey the law. There is no such thing as conscientious objection to law. Civil disobedience is morally wrong. All disagreement with the law is treasonous. State leaders, for example, who brand as traitors those who protest against military draft laws, are following the philosophy of Hobbes. I may never set myself up against the law in the name of higher morality. The law *is* morality. There is no such thing as an unjust law.

16

A less pessimistic view of society is espoused by personalistic and pragmatic philosophies. Love, not law, is the primary value for the personalist. Many proponents of the so-called "new morality" take as their starting point Christ's commandment of love, the first and greatest commandment. When there is a conflict between law (be it religious or civil) and love of my neighbor, choose love. There may be such a thing as an unjust law, a law which violates love. Such laws must be disobeyed in the name of the higher moral law of love. Thus many people feel justified in disobeying in the name of love those laws which foster racial discrimination or war. But love will also demand that laws be obeyed for the good of others and society. Law is not automatically a threat to freedom, as Sartre would say, nor is it automatically to be obeyed, as Hobbes would assert. Love mediates between these extremes.

The pragmatist feels that love is too vague a norm to be of much help. Love whom? My family? My country? Mankind? Suppose there is a conflict between my love of family and my love of country. Which love do I follow? According to the pragmatist, intelligence rather than love has to be the guide. Every moral dilemma is unique. Hence each problem has to be tackled on its own terms. A universal answer like "love" is no help. What I should try to do first is to gather all the data of the problem at hand, much as the scientist lines up the data of his problem before forming a hypothesis for solving it. Suppose, for example, that a soldier is ordered to destroy the homes of what appear to him to be innocent women and children. The fact that sometimes he is commanded to take action which results in the death of innocent people is beginning to seriously bother him as a moral problem. His love of country (obeying his orders as a soldier) is coming into conflict with his love of humanity (the innocent lives he is harming and destroying). The pragmatist says that it is not a case of choosing either law (obedience) or love, nor is it a case of choosing between love of country and love of humanity. Your problem is that you love both. Your solution will try to take *both* loves into account, much as the scientist looks for a hypothesis that will explain *all* his conflicting data, not just some of it. What hypothesis will enable this soldier to go on living with both love of country and love of humanity? Just as the problem differs from person to person, so will the solution differ from person to person. The solution I can live with (this is the pragmatic test) may be different from the solution you could live with. The soldier in question might, for example, continue to obey orders (love of country) but also give what time he can to helping war orphans and refugees (love of humanity). Another might not be able to live with such a solution. He might have to refuse to obey orders (love of humanity) and try to obtain conscientious objector status, prepared to accept all the consequences of this decision (respect for the law of his country). Just as the scientist tests his hypothesis by experiment, so the pragmatist tests his moral solution by his ability to live with it. It is not the vague idea of love which guides his moral life, but intelligence tested by its consequences for his life and the lives of those with whom he is bound up in society.

Therefore, in summary, what is the relation of the individual to society? How are we to understand *sociality* which together with freedom and intelligence forms the core of the philosophy of man in this book? We have seen a wide range of answers. Sartre uncompromisingly asserts the primacy of individual freedom. Hobbes uncompromisingly asserts the supremacy of law. For both, people are natural enemies to one another. There is no natural basis for community among humans. For personalists, there is a natural bond of love which draws men together. This is why love can mediate between freedom and law. Neither is absolute. It is love which is absolute. My individual freedom is fostered by loving my fellows and even by obeying the community's laws. But because love and not law is the basis of community, I can at times disobey the law in the name of love.

For the pragmatist, all sides of a moral conflict must be taken into consideration. Individual freedom may be one part of the conflict, but it should not be made into the whole story. A law might provide another aspect of the conflict in question, but neither should law be made into an absolute answer. Various loves may provide other sides to your moral conflict, but love in general is too vague to be made into a moral absolute. "Knowledge is virtue." Intelligence looks for a solution which takes all sides of the moral conflict into account. I look for a solution which respects the law, maintains my integrity and freedom and tries to do justice to all my loves. My life is an experiment. The solutions I can live with are the good ones. But new problems keep forcing me to new evaluations. Some solutions don't work. They hurt my freedom or make me bypass laws I want to obey or lead me to overlook people I want to love. Thus a new conflict arises and I try again for the intelligent solution which takes all the data into account. This book tends to favor the pragmatic view of society rather than the pessimism of Sartre or Hobbes or the vagueness of the new morality. Sociality as understood by the pragmatists includes both freedom and law and love with intelligence as the guiding norm. Again, with Socrates and Dewey, we assert: "Knowledge is virtue."

4.

What ever happened to the natural law?

THE PROBLEM. The "natural law" concept in Christian ethics has fallen upon hard times. It seems simple enough. God made nature a certain way. He made it that way because he wanted to make it that way. Hence, to learn the laws and purposes of nature is to learn the laws and purposes of God. For example, it seems obvious that the human sexual faculties were made to procreate children. We know this because this is what they do when we use them and do not interfere with their function. If God did not want them to function for this purpose, he would not have made them that way. Therefore, since birth control is against *nature*, it is against the *law* of God. In a word, it is against the *natural law*.

But opponents of this natural law theory wonder if man is meant simply to follow nature like a book in which we can clearly read the will of God. Assuming that God made the winter to be cold, is it against the natural law to build houses with central heating to keep people warm in the winter? Assuming that God made some people with sugar imbalance which leads to diabetes and death, is it against the natural law to take insulin to interfere with the sugar-producing function of the body? Assuming that God made some women with very weak hearts so that further pregnancies would mean death, is it against the natural law to take pills to prevent further pregnancies? In a word, is nature a book for humans to read, or is nature a book for man to write?

THE ISSUES INVOLVED. Clearly at issue here are two different views of nature and two different views of what we should do with nature. Following the principle "Nature is the measure of action," we ask which of these two views best tells the story of the way it is with humans and nature. Is the universe a finished product, an ordered harmonious cosmos reflecting the order and harmony of the divine will? Or is the universe still evolving and unfinished, providing not answers but problems challenging us to intelligently control it for our own purposes?

Before the rise of science, medieval philosophers followed the lead of the ancient Greek philosophers in viewing nature as an ordered whole governed by eternal laws which were already present and operating and just waiting to be discovered. The order of the universe was a proof that the divine intelligence was at work in it, keeping the stars on their courses and ensuring that season would follow season and that the species of bird and animal would continually reproduce themselves, each keeping its fixed and proper place. Human intelligence was a reflection of this divine intelligence in nature. The task of human intelligence was simply to discover the ready-made order of nature put there by the divine intelligence. Having discovered this order, what better could one do than follow it? For this order represented the divine intelligence itself, and hence the divine will. Ethics was thus based on the natural law. This natural law ethics was completely in harmony with man's view of God, nature and human intelligence and represented the best thinking of philosophers and theologians for two thousand years.

The rise of science shattered this view of human intelligence and the evolutionary hypothesis shattered this view of nature. In this new view, nature is far from being finished, far from harmoniously ordered. It is still evolving, still in the making. Species aren't fixed, not even the human species. Humans evolved from other animals, and are evolving still. Since society and the world are changing, new problems constantly arise challenging humans to find new solutions. The laws of human nature, society and the universe are not sitting there waiting to be discovered. The world is evolving and so is human nature. In fact, the human animal is itself determining which way it will evolve. The moral problem of war, for example, is a completely different problem calling for radically different moral solutions in the nuclear age as compared to the age of the bow and arrow. A society which can annihilate itself is a different kind of animal from one which sees itself as passively determined by the will of God. We are now writing the book of nature with the alphabet of space exploration, population control, telstar communications and nuclear research. It's not that we don't want to obey the natural law. There is no passive nature there waiting to be discovered. We are shaping nature to our own purposes. Intelligence has become our instrument of creation and control.

Obviously, these two views of human beings and their relation to nature will give rise to two very different views of natural law and morality. Let's compare what we will call Greek nature and evolving nature. For Greek nature there can be unchanging moral answers. Nature is ever the same; the same moral problems keep recurring and the same answers will hold true. But evolving nature keeps giving rise to new problems challenging man to work out new solutions. For Greek nature, God established an unchanging order so that the order of nature reflects the intelligence and will of God. The order of nature becomes the natural law. But an evolving nature is continually shaped by man in his freedom. Nature reflects the intelligent creativity of man as much as of God. To a great extent the order of nature is a product of man's activity. There is no ready-made natural law.

In Greek nature, the only change in natural law is a change in our mind when we discover in nature something of which we were unaware but which was there all the time. In evolutionary nature, not only our knowledge changes but nature itself is changed by our knowledge. In Greek nature, the moral law is discovered in nature. Nature is a book written by God to be read by humankind. Evolving nature is a book written by humans; their only guide is their own moral responsibility as they try to develop fully what it means to be intelligent, free and social human beings. God may be alive, patting us on the back and encouraging us to use our freedom with confidence and responsibility, but God is certainly dead as far as giving step-by-step answers and directions for the use of freedom. That's what happened to natural law.

You could work out a new theory of natural law more in conformity with nature the way we know it today. Such a theory would have to take into account evolution, science, the effect on the world of man's freedom and the effect on us of changing social structures, as well as suggest a method for coping with this new world in an intelligent and responsible way. In a certain sense this book is an effort in that direction. Our free interaction with the evolving world presents us with several moral problems which we will now proceed to examine briefly, as we seek to determine how in the face of these problems we can do moral justice to man's free and intelligent sociality. It is our hope to assist you in clarifying this question for yourself.

SOME FURTHER READINGS

NOTE: Here, and throughout the rest of the book, a few sample follow-up readings are suggested for each topic. Even to suggest a basic minimum list of titles on the range of topics treated would require a book in itself—a book which, incidentally, would be soon outdated. A tasty sample is all that we intend to give, in the hope that it will prove better than nothing at all.

Charles E. Curran, *Ongoing Revision in Moral Theology* (Notre Dame, Indiana: Fides/Claretian, 1975). Here is an excellent account of the present state of the question on Natural Law ethics.

John Dewey, *Theory of the Moral Life* (New York: Holt Rinehart and Winston; paperbound edition, 1966). This is a classic on the pragmatic approach to morals.

Joseph Fletcher, *Situation Ethics: The New Morality* (Philadelphia: Westminster Press; paperbound edition, 1966). Here is a theory of love-based morality by the new morality's most prominent spokesman.

Daniel C. Maguire, *The Moral Choice* (New York: Doubleday and Co., Inc., 1978). This is a nuanced up-to-date discussion of the moral implications of modern ethical theories.

PART II

War at Home and Abroad

5.

Is war a moral way of solving disputes between nations?

> I have known war as few men now living know it.... Its very destructiveness on both friend and foe alike has rendered it useless as a means of settling international disputes.
>
> General Douglas MacArthur[1]

> I have left the privileges and duties of the clergy, but I have not left the priesthood. I believe that I have devoted myself to the revolution out of love for my neighbor.... When my neighbor has nothing against me, when I have realized the revolution, I will then say the Holy Mass again.
>
> Father Camille Torres[2]

THE PROBLEM. There is no sane person who doesn't see war as a problem and an evil. But is war really a *moral* problem for me, the *individual?* One might contend: "I don't make big decisions of war and peace. Only the government has the information and the ability to weigh such issues, so I leave it to them."

But we cannot duck the question so easily. Even the ordinary citizen judges that some wars are clearly unjust. This is why after World War II the Allies at Nuremburg condemned citizens for not recognizing the unjust conduct of their government and for not refusing to cooperate with that government. A nation is made up of all the citizens; it is not just the government. Here we can recall sociologist Peter Berger's observation that the biggest illusion of all grown-ups is the idea that there is a world of adults out there somewhere who really understand what's going

---

[1]Quoted from the War Resisters' League pamphlet, *G.I. or C.O.*
[2]Quoted from *The Religious Situation 1968* (Boston: Beacon Press, 1968), p. 507.

on and are taking care of everything. The fact is that we are all responsible for muddling along together.

In the question of war, for example, each of us is responsible for either espousing or protesting or silently consenting to a given war policy. Each of us pays taxes which support an army and buy rifles, napalm and nuclear weapons. Each of us is responsible for whom we vote into office, for contributing to a war economy and for accepting the benefits of a nation's strong defense. Finally, some are responsible for actually bearing arms and killing other human beings. We are all cooperators. Is this cooperation good or evil?

ARGUMENTS FOR AND AGAINST. We can break up the moral question of war into two parts. The first question is: Can war ever be a moral way of settling international disputes? Absolute pacifists answer: "No, never!" However, most people are relative pacifists, and their attitude is: "It depends." If you grant that war can sometimes be just, the second question then arises: How do I tell the difference between a just and an unjust war?

In stark and simple terms, the issue between absolute pacifists and others turns on two points: a value judgment and a moral principle. The heart of the pacifist ethic is an exquisite reverence for human life and the supreme value, a value to be cherished on this earth above all other values. It is unthinkable that there could be a "good reason" for the organized, systematic, large-scale killing which is war. To engage in mass destruction in the name of freedom, or of God and country, or of defense, or of democracy is sheer illusion. War's mass slaughter destroys the very values which it claims to be vindicating. "We had to destroy the village in order to save it"—this sentiment is, for the pacifist, the supreme irony of all war. Human life is a value which takes second place to no other. It is no accident that humanists are the most ardent pacifists.

Opponents of absolute pacifism take a wider view of human life, and in their opinion they have a more realistic approach to the moral dilemma of war. After all, they say, everybody dies sooner or later both in peace and in war, and death is the gateway to another life. The believer in immortality is less likely to take the earthly span of life as an *ultimate* value. It is no accident that Christians have not been noted for pacifism. But leaving immortality aside, we can still take a wider view of human life than sheer physical existence. For when the political, economic and social conditions for human spiritual growth are lacking, then human life scarcely exceeds that of the brute. Hence, sometimes war and revolution are the only way to achieve decent food and lodging, the opportunity for education or the freedom to worship. Without these, human life isn't worth living. War and revolution are sometimes a necessary evil.

This brings us to the second point which separates pacifists from others—namely, the application of the moral principle of choosing the lesser of two evils. This principle is a simple maxim of intelligence. It states that when you are confronted with just two alternatives, both of which are evil, you must choose the lesser evil. It certainly wouldn't be smart, and hence it wouldn't be moral either, to choose the greater evil! Accordingly, there are times when a nation is in the grip of tyranny or under attack, and all peaceful attempts at solution have failed. Faced with a choice between the evil of tyranny and enemy destruction or the evil of revolution and war, revolution and war are the lesser evil. In such a case I would be morally obliged to fight.

The absolute pacifist, in answer to this argument, does not deny the principle of choosing the lesser of two evils when faced with only two alternatives, both of which are evil. What the absolute pacifist denies is that we are ever faced with only evil alternatives in the case of war. There is always a good alternative course of action which we can choose—namely, the alternative of *non-violent resistance* to evil. When you have a good alternative, it is neither intelligent nor moral to choose even a lesser evil. You choose the good—namely, non-violent resistance.

To the assertion that non-violent resistance is unrealistic, the pacifist will answer that it has never really been tried. Certainly war has not been the way to peace. "There is no way to peace; peace is the way." Peaceful resistance to evil should not be misunderstood. It is really *resistance*. It does not mean being a doormat. It means standing up for what you believe, urging it, acting for it, organizing for it, sabotaging and thwarting evil in every possible way short of destroying human life. For to take life is to fall victim to the same evil you claim to be fighting.

Non-violent resistance intends to change the rules of the war game. War is a contest to see who can be the most inhuman and brutal. Whoever succeeds in being the most destructive is declared the victor. Massive non-violent resistance, on the other hand, operates on the supposition that the enemy is human too. Certainly non-violent resisters will be killed. But the enemy, being human, will be unable to slaughter indefinitely other human beings who persistently refuse to retaliate in kind. The enemy's humanity will break through and he will cease to kill. Such is the pacifist's act of faith in human beings. Instead of a contest of inhumanity, the non-violent resister wins by being more human. While many people will die, probably fewer will do so than would in a war. And above all, the quality of death is different. These deaths are witnesses to the value of non-violent love, and not the result of a contest in brutality.

Is non-violent resistance practical? The pacifist replies that we don't know for sure, since it has never been tried on a massive scale with the same budget, education and propaganda that war has enjoyed. We do know without the slightest uncertainty that war has failed to bring peace. And from the more modest experiments in non-violence we have some hint of its power. "The blood of martyrs is the seed of Christians"—this is a pragmatic maxim!

ISSUES TO BE RESOLVED. 1. Is war ever a moral means for solving international disputes? Your answer depends on the position you take on the following issues:

(a) Is earthly human life an absolute value, so that the organized destruction of life entailed by war could never be justified for any reason?

(b) Is the alternative of non-violent resistance always possible, so that the principle of the lesser of two evils cannot be invoked in the case of war?

(c) Or, on the other hand, must we sometimes "destroy the village in order to save it?" In other words, do values such as the opportunity for subsistence, education and worship sometimes outweigh the value of human life, and hence justify its destruction in revolution or in war? If the answer is affirmative, then could non-violent resistance itself be the greater evil, and hence sometimes immoral?

2. If war can sometimes be moral, how can I tell the differ-

ence between a just and an unjust war? A just war is one which is really the least evil of all the alternative courses of action. Some considerations would be:

(a) Is there a proportion between the goals I hope to attain and the evils inflicted on combatants and innocents? (The destructive potential of modern weaponry is a major factor here: napalm is a long way from the bow and arrow.)

(b) Have all peaceful alternatives been exhausted?

(c) Could I avoid war and achieve a better preponderance of good over evil by being satisfied with more moderate and gradual goals?

(d) What is the proportion between present evil and the danger of evil in the future? Would war now prevent an even greater war in the future, or vice versa?

AN OPINION. Three dimensions of the war question deserve more thought than is usually given to them. First, we are too quick to think immediately in terms of the war game and of the politics of brute power. War is a battle for people's minds and hearts. Does brute power change people's hearts? Which has won over more people—napalm bombing or Peace Corps service? While it is difficult to be a total pacifist, the pacifist ethic can keep us from reverting too quickly to the framework of the war game.

Second, and in the opposite direction from pacifism, is there an irradicable irrational streak in human nature which makes war inevitable? Perhaps we are burdened with an aggressive instinct which removes the war question from the area of reason and morality. Could it be that aggression is necessary for the survival of the human animal? In this hypothesis, while talk of rationality and non-violence might apply to some other species, it wouldn't apply to humans.

Third, are the values for which people fight really human values? I wonder what my humanity has to do with the kind of food I eat, where national boundaries are drawn, whether I worship in church or at home, or how politicians and soldiers choose to strut about. Why are human institutions, destined to be outmoded in a few decades, worth the mass slaughter of human beings?

SOME FURTHER READINGS

Konrad Lorenz, *On Aggression* (New York: Harcourt, 1966; Bantam paperbound, 1967). This is a remarkably interesting study of aggression in the fish, bird and animal kingdoms, leading up to an evaluation of the aggressive instinct as it appears in the human animal.

Gordon Zahn, *An Alternative to War* (Pamphlet published by the Council for Religion and International Affairs in New York City). Here is a powerful presentation of the case for absolute pacifism.

6.

Does the conscientious objector (the C.O.) fail in his duty to his country?

That military service in this country's armed forces is an option exercisable solely at the discretion of the individual: no nation anywhere, now or in the past, has ever recognized that principle. Those who urge individual defiance on moral grounds merely betray the genuine tenets of conscientious objection which our people respect.

Freedom House Statement[1]

If my soldiers began to think, not one would remain in the ranks.

Frederick the Great[2]

THE PROBLEM. Whatever one thinks of war, it is impossible not to face the question of conscientious objection to war. The C.O. is a deviant in society, condemned by the established order. Society is tempted to dismiss the C.O. as stupid, condemn him as immoral, or even punish him as criminal. The nub of the moral problem here is the relation of the individual to society—in this case, to his country. On what basis could an individual intelligently and morally stand up against his country? Is such a stance reconcilable with his duty to country? How should society view the C.O.? How does the C.O. view society?

ARGUMENTS FOR AND AGAINST. The main argument against conscientious objection turns on the social nature of human beings. "No man is an island." No one can pretend in the

---

[1]Statement of the Freedom House Foundation, quoted in *Worldview* (February 1967), p. 2.
[2]Quoted from the War Resisters' League pamphlet, *G.I. or C.O.*

name of conscience to act as if he didn't owe his existence, his education, his well-being and his freedom to the society which nurtured him or her and continues to nurture him—in this case, to his country. All patriotism is not chauvinistic. It is a fact of life that the C.O.'s very freedom to object is protected by those against whom he is objecting, and furthermore it is being protected by force of arms, the very point of the C.O.'s objection. The C.O. wants to have his cake and eat it too, continues the argument. Conscientious objectors condemn their society as if they were isolated individuals but at the very same time they are reaping all the benefits of being part of that society. Such blindness to one's social nature and duty is unintelligent and immoral. To enjoy the benefits of society implies the duty to fight for it. If you don't want to conform, get out.

In reply, conscientious objectors contend that they are social beings, but that they are first of all citizens of the society of humankind. To this society belongs not only their own nation but the enemy's nation as well. No country has the right to ask them to unjustly kill their fellow human beings. Our common humanity is what most profoundly unites us all.

The *absolute pacifist* will be a universal C.O. Such people object to all war since there is no such thing as a just war. They will be consistent in refusing to cooperate in any way with their country's military machine. The *relative pacifist* will be a selective C.O. Such people refuse to kill fellow human beings in an unjust war in the name of patriotism, but are willing to fight in a just war.

Both C.O. and patriot (the C.O. is patriotic too; I'm using the word here in the narrow sense) agree that human nature is social. The C.O. contends that the society of human beings is primary, and it is on the basis of membership in the human race that the C.O. is morally justified in standing up against the lesser national society. The patriot contends that it is the nation, and not mankind, that confers nurture, freedom and protection on the citizen—hence duty to one's country comes first.

Some seek to compromise by refusing military service but accepting an alternate assignment, thus reconciling duty to country and duty to mankind. As a human being such a compromise objector refuses to bear arms in an unjust war, but as a patriot he will perform non-combatant service. The absolute C.O. will accuse the compromise objector of indirectly fostering the war he pretends to protest. The patriot will accuse him of refusing to fight for the nation which supports him.

ISSUES TO BE RESOLVED. We have seen three different approaches to resolving a conflict between individual conscience and society, illustrated by the solutions of the patriot, the absolute objector and the compromise objector. Really, three different moralities are involved: (1) an ontological morality (in which the individual accepts society the way he finds it); (2) a prophetic morality (in which the individual attempts to change society according to his ideals); (3) a pragmatic morality (in which the individual attempts a compromise between his ideals and the actual situation). The moral decision you make regarding conscientious objection will depend to a great extent upon which of these three moralities guides your moral thinking.

1. The patriot is ontological: "Accept the society you live in. It comes first. There is no higher base from which to oppose it."

2. The absolute objector is a prophet: "If a society commands immorality, you must oppose it. There is no compromise with evil and certainly no justification for acquiescence in it."

3. The compromise objector is pragmatic: "Pay heed to individual conscience by objecting, and hence trying to change society. However, also pay heed to your society by serving it, even though it is involved in evil. Without surrendering to evil, you must learn to live with it."

AN OPINION. Society needs all three moral vocations. It needs those who conform and cooperate (fortunately, perhaps, the majority), those who revolutionize and reform, and those who compromise the ideal with the actual order of things. For most of us there are some evils with which we compromise, others we readily accept, and still others against which we rebel. In the last analysis it comes down to asking what decision one can live with as an intelligent and moral human being. Maybe a prophet couldn't live with himself unless he protested evil to the point of imprisonment, whereas a father of ten children could be equally driven to compromise.

SOME FURTHER READINGS

Saul D. Alinsky, *Rules for Radicals: A Pragmatic Primer for Realistic Radicals* (New York: Vintage Books, 1972).

Joan V. Bondurant, *Conquest of Violence: The Gandhian Philosophy of Conflict* (Berkeley: University of California Press, revised edition, 1965).

Robert S. Rivkin and Barton F. Stichman, *The Rights of Military Personnel: An ACLU Handbook* (New York: Avon Books, 1977).

7.

What about civil disobedience? Can people pick and choose what laws they will obey?

"Please would you tell me—" she began, looking timidly at the Red Queen.

"Speak when you're spoken to!" the Queen sharply interrupted her.

"But if everybody obeyed that rule," said Alice who was always ready for a little argument, "and if you only spoke when you were spoken to, and the other person always waited for you to begin, you see nobody would ever say anything, so that—"

"Ridiculous!" replied the Queen. "Why, don't you see, child"—here she broke off with a frown, and after thinking for a minute, suddenly changed the topic of conversation.

Lewis Carroll, *Through the Looking Glass*

... that the State may prevent any conduct which induces people to violate the law, or any advocacy of unlawful activity, cannot be squared with the First Amendment.

U.S. Supreme Court, *Musser vs. Utah*[1]

THE PROBLEM. Anarchy is the end result of systematic planned disobedience of law, and yet this is exactly what civil disobedience is: breaking the law in an organized strategic way. How does the civil objector differ from the anarchist? How from the criminal? Once again we are faced with the tension between the individual and the laws of society which seem unjust. Like conscientious objection, civil disobedience is an attempt to re-

[1]Quoted from the Fund for the Republic's pamphlet on *Civil Disobedience*, p. 8.

form society into the shape of one's own ideals. But not all conscientious objection is civil disobedience. When conscientious objectors object within the law (e.g., applying for and receiving C.O. status), they are obeying the law. They are not being civilly disobedient. On the other hand, not all disobedience of the law is civil disobedience. For example, if someone hides his identity and runs away in order to evade the draft and escape punishment for evasion, he is not being civilly disobedient but criminally disobedient.

Civil disobedience differs from criminal disobedience of the law in two ways. First, civil disobedience is public, whereas criminal disobedience is private and hidden; second, the person who civilly disobeys the law stands ready to accept the legal consequences of his act, whereas the criminal seeks to evade legal punishment. These two differences stem from the purpose of civil disobedience. Civil disobedience is public because it seeks by this act to call attention to an unjust law: its purpose is educational. And civil disobedience stands ready to accept the legal consequences because this readiness bears witness to its respect for law and order. Civil disobedience does not reject the legal system but rather seeks to make it just. Hence the disobedience is carried out entirely within the framework of the legal system. For example, to publicly burn one's draft card with readiness to accept the consequences would be an act of civil disobedience.

ARGUMENTS FOR AND AGAINST. Arguments against civil disobedience miss the point when they are based on the civil objector's alleged disrespect for the law. This is to confuse it with criminal disobedience. As we have seen, the goal of civil disobedience is not to break down the rule of law but to make it more just, not to seek private gain, but public education, and not to evade the consequences of the law but to accept them.

Civil disobedience is a strategy of reform. More powerful are the arguments leveled against it as a poor strategy, a strategy which does more harm than good. First, civil disobedience *is* illegal, albeit for the best of motives. Is it not preferable, is it not the lesser evil, that reform take place within the legally constituted institutions of change in a society? Secondly, civil disobedience teaches the wrong lesson. The mass of society misses the noble purpose and sees only the disobedience. Hence most people will be impelled by example to disobey the laws that *they* don't like. Like it or not, disrespect for law and order is the lesson taught by civil disobedience. Third, civil disobedience doesn't work. People's consciences are stirred to contempt rather than to reform. They say: "I'd like to pick and choose my laws." They don't ask: "What injustice are these people pointing out to me."

The civil objector rightly points out that these arguments are based on misunderstanding. But he also realizes that civil disobedience's whole purpose is to communicate understanding. Civil disobedience that is misunderstood is an exercise in futility. Hence there is the heavy responsibility on the civil objector to make perfectly clear not only his act but the philosophy lying behind it.

ISSUES TO BE RESOLVED. The arguments raised against civil disobedience as a strategy challenge the civil objector to resolve the following issues in coming to his decision:

1. Does the injustice which is protested outweigh the damage done to the social structure by the illegality of the protest? On the face of it, illegality is an evil. It must be shown to be the lesser evil.

2. Is the illegal protest creating a climate of disrespect for law as it pursues its intended effect of pointing out injustice? Does my hope of communicating the good lesson balance out the risk of communicating the bad lesson?

3. Is this the most effective means of public education that I can use? Will it be an irritant that will more probably create opposition than lead to reform?

AN OPINION. Civil disobedience as an educational technique relies to a great extent on its novelty and unexpectedness for its impact. Its effectiveness is greatly blunted when it becomes routine, expected, almost institutionalized. Once this happens, civil disobedience becomes more therapeutic for the demonstrator than for the society it is trying to reform. Then we are left with recourse to two ways of correcting injustice: either due legal process within the political system or violent revolution outside and against the political system. This latter alternative is considered next.

SOME FURTHER READINGS

Elizabeth Janeway, *Powers of the Weak* (New York: Alfred A. Knopf, 1980).

Gene Sharp, *The Politics of Nonviolent Action* (Boston: Potter, Sargent, Publishers, 1973).

8.

Is violent protest always evil even though it has
a good purpose?

> Men can live without justice and generally must, but
> they cannot live without hope.
>
> Eric Hobsbawm[1]

> Terrorism is theater.
>
> Elizabeth Janeway[2]

THE PROBLEM. Despair about the possibility of effecting
meaningful change through political means has led to the advocacy of domestic violence. This is a relatively new phenomenon
on the American scene. Robert Kennedy once said that acceptance of violence abroad leads to its acceptance at home. As trag-
ically as events have borne this out, still the parallel is not
perfect. International violence or war has been accepted in lieu
of an effective political forum for settling all international disputes. But political institutions do exist for settling internal disputes in a democratic country. We will confine ourselves to the
question of violence in a democratic society, since this is the
more difficult question. Why is it that more and more people not
only resort to violence on the domestic scene but advocate it as
intelligent and moral?

Many people now despair of the effectiveness of non-violent
civil disobedience as a strategy for change. Far from condemnations of civil disobedience as containing the seeds of anarchy, we
now hear that it is not anarchical enough. Civil disobedience respects established law and seeks to reform it, not to overthrow
it. For the advocates of violence, established law is evil; there can
be no working within it or any compromise. It must be over-

---

[1]Eric Hobsbawm, *Bandits* (New York: Delacorte Press, 1969), p. 43.
[2]Janeway, *op.cit.*, p. 227.

turned. The established public has become immune to the message of civil disobedience, but the message of violence comes in loud and clear.

Is violence automatically immoral? Are life and property always morally inviolable? Indeed, is it morally unthinkable that the established political, economic and social system of a country should be overthrown?

ARGUMENTS FOR AND AGAINST. The basic issue here is the morality of revolution. When does the established power become so intransigent in its evil that the only moral alternative is to overthrow it? "Positive thinking" continues to hope for reform from within the system. "The power of negative thinking" (as Herbert Marcuse calls it) is to challenge the system from the outside by intellectual revolt, and in the extremity by violent physical revolt.

We are accustomed to thinking of revolution in relation to political tyranny, as a revolt against an absolute monarch or dictator. But the "free world" lives in an environment dominated by mass communications whose purse-strings are controlled by industry, and under a government whose purse-strings are controlled by the military-industrial complex; thus it is living under a tyranny more absolute than any medieval prince or petty modern dictator could devise.

In such an atmosphere, the revolutionist argument continues, effective dissent within the system is impossible, although the outward trappings of dissent are indeed possible. Every opinion, however stupid, has its day in court. Truth and falsehood, intellectual acuity and obtuseness have the same pedestal. "Equal time" brings all opinion to the same level. Thus the mass media neutralize dissent, blunting the sharp tooth that would tear aside its pretensions. Meanwhile, the military-industrial complex, by judiciously allotting funds, ensures its own perpetuation. This is the tyranny of pragmatism, the philosophy which compromises with the situation as it is. What is called for is revolution, the overthrow of a system that perpetuates its own evil. Such is the main thrust of the revolutionist argument for violence in a democratic society. Obviously, a prophetic morality is at work here.

To the objection that reform can be gradually brought about if one works patiently within the system, the revolutionary replies that people don't grow up gradually over the centuries. They grow up in minutes, days and years. The evil is now; the evil being done to me and my children cannot be changed when I and they are dead. Though on paper democracy allows for change, in practice there is no leeway for change within the system.

ISSUES TO BE RESOLVED. The morality of revolution involves many issues already considered in connection with war, conscientious objection and civil disobedience. The following issues are relevant to an intelligent and moral evaluation of the revolutionist's project in particular.

1. Assuming that there exists a serious social evil calling for reform, is this evil so firmly entrenched in the established system that the only hope of correcting it is in the overthrow of the system?

2. If so, are the evils of overthrowing the system less than the evils of trying to work within it? What will society look like after the revolution? This issue is most often ignored.

AN OPINION. People tend to condemn the terrorist on moral grounds. To be sure, terrorist violence is morally repugnant. But to focus on the violence is to miss the point. The contest is not between an immoral band of outlaws and the moral majority of citizens. Rather the contest is between two moralities: the morality of the established regime and the morality of the new order envisioned by the revolutionary group. Violent acts are dramatic gestures designed to draw the attention of the citizenry to the revolutionary cause and ideals. The deeper moral issue is not the terrorist violence, but the perceived injustice that fires the revolutionaries and the new moral order they would create.

SOME FURTHER READINGS

Edward H. Price, "The Strategy and Tactics of Revolutionary Terrorism," in *Comparative Studies in Society and History* (January 1977).

John Wheeler-Bennett, *Friends, Enemies and Sovereigns* (London: Macmillan and Co., 1976).

PART III

Moral Control over Life and Health

9.

Is abortion murder? How do we know when life begins?

> If men could get pregnant, abortion would be a sacrament.
>
> Florynce Kennedy[1]

> Most doctors feel that there is even something unwholesome and unsavory about therapeutic abortion. Whatever it may do for the mother, they know it obviously can't be very therapeutic for the baby.
>
> Dr. Herbert Ratner[2]

THE PROBLEM. Abortion is among the most discussed of this next cluster of issues concerned with care of life and health. It is not the law but the morality of abortion that we are discussing here. For the common good you could easily support a relaxed abortion law, while morally rejecting abortion for yourself. What kind of killing does abortion involve? Is it merely another kind of contraception? Or, on the other hand, do foeticide and infanticide come down to the same thing? What reasons could justify the direct killing of an inviable foetus (i.e., a foetus which cannot survive outside of the womb)? Abortion is murder if there is no such reason. Otherwise, abortion could be justifiable killing.

ARGUMENTS FOR AND AGAINST. Is the foetus merely an organ of the mother which she might remove, like her tonsils, if she had a reason (e.g., she might not want another baby: this is the most common reason for seeking an abortion)? Or is the foetus human? If human, when does the foetus become a human being? Spiritualists assert that the foetus becomes human when it

[1]Rowes, *op.cit,* p. 29.
[2]*Catholic Mind* (May 1966), p. 46.

receives its soul. Since souls are invisible, this unfortunately isn't much help. Foetuses start to *look* human after three months, more so after six months, more so still after birth. Infants start to *act* human as they approach their first birthday, and even more so as they approach the age of reason. It is pretty evident that we do not know any magic moment when the genetic material suddenly leaps from prehuman to human status. In the face of this despair of discovering such a magic moment, the traditionalists say: "Play it safe; act *as if* the foetus were human from the very first instant of conception: it might be human, so you can't take the chance of killing it." The reformers say: "Though we are not sure that the foetus is human, we are sure that the parents are, so for their own good reasons they may morally decide on abortion."

Both of these extreme positions pretend to know nothing of the humanity of the foetus. One says blindly: "Play it safe"; the other says blindly: "Do what you will." But are we really all that blind? We know nothing of magic moments, but we do know that from the moment of conception till the moment of death there is a progressive evolutionary development toward ever fuller and richer human function, appearance, life and behavior.

The first critical moment in every human being's evolutionary life span is the moment of his conception where there is formed the completely unique genetic package from which he is to develop. The final critical moment of a human's observable development is the moment of death which capitulates and climaxes all that he has become as a human being. In between the minimal humanity of the newly formed zygote and the maximal humanity of the surrender of the adult organism at death, there lies a continuous line of ever-growing humanness. And along this line of development certain critical stages can be pointed out. First, there is fertilization. Several days later the zygote is activated to start developing in an irreversibly humanoid direction. A next critical point would be the zygote's implantation on the wall of the uterus when the cells are differentiated, some developing into the placenta and others evolving into the foetus. Succeeding critical stages in a progressively more human direction might be pointed out: the period when organs and limbs take on recognizable shape, the stage when the foetus becomes viable, the moment of actual birth, the stage when the child begins to

speak, the stage when the child begins to exercise moral auton-
omy, the age of puberty, marriage, the stage of parenthood, etc.,
up till the moment of death.

Clearly in the light of these data, any decision to have an
abortion must take into account the evolving human life which
is being ended. While the zygote at the moment of conception
may not have the full status and rights of an adult human, it is
clearly not just an organ of the mother's body. Any reason offered for abortion must weigh in the balance the independently
evolving human life which is destroyed. Would birth control justify killing the foetus? Would the health of the mother? Would
the life of the mother?

ISSUES TO BE RESOLVED. Your moral decision regarding
abortion will depend on your view of the humanity of the foetus.
If the foetus is simply an organ of the mother's body (a medically
dubious proposition), then no greater reason would be needed for
an abortion than for any other operation involving an organ ex-
cision. If the foetus is presumed to be a fully human person from
the first instant of conception, then the killing of the foetus may
no more be justified than the killing of an adult human. Of
course, moral arguments are devised to justify killing humans in
war, in self-defense, in punishment for crimes or in the case of
mercy killings. Parallels can be worked out to justify abortion,
even on the presumption that the foetus is fully human.

The third view regards the foetus as neither merely an organ nor yet fully human, but as an evolving human life with rights
which in some evolving degree flow from this fact. As the foetus
develops, more serious reasons would be needed to justify termination of the pregnancy. In this view, for example, the termination of a pregnancy by taking the so-called "morning after" birth
control pill would be a different kind of case from ending the life
of a four-month-old foetus for reasons of birth control. Evolving
foetal life means evolving foetal rights.

AN OPINION. A great number of pro-abortion arguments pretend to be concerned with the alleged unhappiness which would
be the lot of the prospective child. Usually, the more honest reason for abortions is the attempt to avoid unhappiness for the
mother in having an "unwanted" child. Would you rather be

46

"unwanted" or dead? I have often thought it would be only courtesy to let the child grow old enough to answer this question, and do away with the little tacker only after he chooses death. A similar honesty would be refreshing in the cases of abortion when there is danger of the birth of a defective child. Granting the morality of euthanasia, wouldn't it be more intelligent to wait until after the birth of the child to ascertain with certainty whether or not the child is defective? And again, the question could be put: Would you rather be defective or dead? Aren't you just a little defective?

SOME FURTHER READINGS

John R. Connery, S.J., *Abortion: The Development of the Roman Catholic Perspective* (Chicago: Loyola University Press, 1977).

James C. Mohr, *Abortion in America: The Origins and Evolution of National Policy* (New York: Oxford University Press, 1978).

Susan Teft Nicholson, *Abortion and the Roman Catholic Church* (Knoxville: Religious Ethics, Inc., 1978).

John T. Noonan, Jr., *The Morality of Abortion: Legal and Historical Perspectives* (Cambridge: Harvard University Press, 1970.)

10.

Is my life in my own hands? May I shorten my life by the use of tobacco and alcohol? May I experiment with it by using mind-altering drugs? May I end it by consenting to euthanasia? Must I prolong it as far as possible? May I commit suicide?

The goal of all life is death.

Sigmund Freud[1]

The trust of medicine is the wholeness of life. Its commitment is to keep the flame of life burning, not its embers glimmering. . . . It is ultimately the concept of *life,* not the concept of death which rules the question of the "right to die."

Hans Jonas[2]

THE PROBLEM. The issue in this question is post-foetal life—your life. Is there life after birth? How do you use this one life you have? Alcoholism and euthanasia, the "living will" and the use of nicotine ("an alkaloid poison"), drug abuse and suicide—all challenge you to think about your life and how you use or morally abuse it. The concept of *life* brings these seemingly diverse questions into a single focus.

What rights do we have over the disposition of our own lives? Is my life totally from the hands of God so that I may do nothing with it on my own? Or is my life totally my own so that I may dispose of it as I please? Or is my life not only my own, but the community's too, since I owe a response to the community which bore and nurtured me?

[1]Quoted in Norman Brown, *Life Against Death,* p. 99.
[2]Hans Jonas, "The Right to Die", in Thomas Shannon (ed.), *Bioethics* (Ramsey, N.J.: Paulist Press, 1981), p. 208.

ARGUMENTS FOR AND AGAINST. Once again, the extreme positions afford little moral difficulty. If God controls our lives, then we must submit to his control. However, quite evidently our lives are in our own hands. It is my moral decision whether I work myself to an early grave or pamper my life into coddled longevity. But a freedom that is moral is not arbitrary freedom. I am not morally free to cut off my life at my whim or to use it in any way I please. My life is my own, but it belongs to others as well. Answers to two questions would provide moral guidelines for the use of my life. First, what is this life which I may use or abuse? Secondly, what use or abuse may I make of it? Can I set up a proportion between the life which I have to use and the care and use I may make of it?

All humans are not equal. One human life differs from another, and so does the moral obligation for the care and use of life. There is a great difference between the vegetable life of a permanently comatose, terminally ill, totally senile elderly lady and the hopeful potential of the bubblingly energetic, brightly intelligent little girl. As a one-celled zygote differs from a newborn babe, so does vegetable senility differ from youthful hope. The quality of human life differs, and, accordingly, so do the norms in each case differ as to the reasonable care and prolongation of that human life. The extraordinary drugs and operations which might be morally demanded to save the life of the girl could be totally out of place, unintelligent and immoral if brought to bear in the case of the terminal vegetable-human.

There are two extremes: (1) "There can be no tampering with human life: it comes from God" (this natural law argument just doesn't fit the facts; we do a hundred things a day to prolong and shorten our lives); (2) "Your life is totally in your own hands; do with it what you will" (this Sartrean type argument ignores man's sociality; I am responsible to others and to myself as to how I use my life). We suggest a moral guideline to mediate between these extremes: The means you use to prolong your life should be proportioned to the use you hope to make of it; the means used to shorten life may be in inverse proportion to the use you can reasonably hope to make of your life.

ISSUES TO BE RESOLVED. If neither a blind reliance on God nor a blind personal decision rules the use of my life, then it must be guided by intelligent norms. Where do alcohol, tobacco, pot, L.S.D., heroin, euthanasia and suicide fit on the scale of life and its care and prolongation? We have not the space to give each of these topics the detailed consideration that it deserves. Each demands a careful weighing and balancing out of both good and bad effects—e.g., the euphoria of pot smoking vs. the risk of legal punishment and danger of psychological addiction, the expanded perception in an L.S.D. trip vs. the danger of psychosis or genetic damage, the pain relief from narcotics vs. the danger of permanent addiction. No action is an unmitigated good or evil; bad effects are mingled with good. Intelligent morality strives for a balance in favor of good.

A common thread links all these topics together morally. Each involves an action affecting my health and life (be it taking a glass of beer, an L.S.D. trip or a lethal dose of sleeping pills). Each involves a judgment about the kind of human life affected—e.g., are we talking about a healthy child, a sick adult or a comatose human vegetable? It is not enough to consider the *action* alone, or the *kind of life* alone, but the *relation* between the two. The greater the life potential, the more fear you have of hurting it and the greater effort you put into preserving it. Some examples might clarify this kind of moral thinking.

Among two-pack-a-day smokers, the annual lung cancer rate is seventeen times that of non-smokers. Yet, while it would be recklessly immoral to allow your eight-year-old son to smoke two packs a day, wouldn't you be perfectly intelligent and moral in urging grandpa to smoke to his heart's content?

Or again, while it would be intelligent and moral to spare no medical expense to save a desperately ill young mother of four children, it could be immoral to plunge a whole family into debt to prolong for a month the life of your terminally ill great-grand-uncle.

Or again, while only a moral monster would let her infant daughter starve to death in her crib, it could be a very moral act to remove the intravenous feeding tubes from a horribly suffering, incurable cancer patient. It is the *relation* between the action and the kind of life which is crucial in each case.

AN OPINION. When dealing with abortion, we saw that there is no magic moment in which human life begins. At the other extreme, we can say that there is no magic moment when human life ends. Every day we die a little, and we are all definitely terminal cases! It is no mere figure of speech to say that I "kill myself" for my work, my family, my fun, my friends. Every hour of needed sleep lost, every ounce of alcohol, every cigarette, every straining of muscle and tensing of nerves is a small, nonlethal, gradual suicide. There is no escape. I literally *spend* my life purchasing the good I hope to do. When there is no more good I can hope to do, then I can morally and intelligently spend my last cent. Voluntary euthanasia could well be the final lethal dose culminating a lifetime of non-lethal gradual suicides. And like all the gradual suicides, it will be moral if it is intelligent, i.e., if it is the best balance I can make between my life potential and the care I exercise over it. In other words, while a person may not morally end his life arbitrarily as he will, still we suggest that voluntary euthanasia can sometimes be morally justified.

SOME FURTHER READINGS

Dennis H. Horan and David Mall (eds.), *Death, Dying and Euthanasia* (Washington, D.C.: University Publications of America, 1977).

Vernon Johnson, *I'll Quit Tomorrow: A Practical Guide to Alcoholism Treatment* (New York: Harper and Row, 1980).

Elisabeth Kübler-Ross, *Death, the Final Stage of Growth* (Englewood Cliffs, N.J.: Prentice-Hall, Inc., 1975).

Stanton Peele and Archie Brodsky, *Love and Addiction* (New York: New American Library, 1975).

11.

What is the ethics of the new "baby-making" technologies?

> When you're at the clinic being inseminated, you don't actually comprehend what is going on. You see the syringe and you have to remind yourself, "Gee, there's a baby in there." And then you have to lie there on the table for 10 minutes after they do it with this strange sperm in you, but you think about other things. It does melt out of your mind in daily living. But you're going to go through your life knowing you did this, knowing that there's somebody out there who's part of you somehow.
>
> Young married woman[1]

> What I would say to a child is that it doesn't matter whose uterus you grow in, it matters who takes care of you afterward.
>
> Dr. Lee Salk[2]

THE PROBLEM. Artificial conception has taken center stage away from artificial contraception as a moral issue for the eighties. The new reproductive technologies include *in vitro* or test-tube fertilization. The birth of baby Louise Brown in 1978 transformed the field of human reproduction. Just as artificial contraception makes it possible to have sex without babies, so artificial conception proved it possible to have babies without sex. Woman and man donate egg and sperm. They need not be together at all.

Less dramatic, but more common is the growing phenomenon of surrogate motherhood. A child conceived by artificial in-

[1] Anne Taylor Fleming, "New Frontiers in Conception," *The New York Times Magazine* (July 20, 1980), 14.
[2] *Ibid.*, 52.

semination of a woman who is not his wife is surrendered to the husband and the wife after it is carried to term by this "third party" surrogate mother.

And most common of all is the artificial insemination of women by third party donors (A.I.D.) usually because their husbands or partners are infertile. These third party donors might appropriately be called surrogate fathers. Some 20,000 babies a year in this country owe their existence to A.I.D. So A.I.D. is not an insignificant phenomenon.

What is the ethics of manufacturing human life? How moral is it to separate procreation so radically from the physical act of love?

ARGUMENTS FOR AND AGAINST. Clearly these technologies bring joy and fulfillment to parents who long for children and cannot have them in the ordinary way. This is the strongest argument in favor of such procedures. They represent science at its best, serving human beings by assisting nature when nature on its own can't do the job.

This research, too, is vastly expanding our knowledge about human conception and foetal growth. This serves the quality of human life, bringing genetic defects under better control and improving prenatal foetal care. The upshot is healthier pregnancies and people with fewer defects. All this is obvious and good.

Serious questions remain, however. First, all these procedures fall heir to the same objections as levelled against artificial contraception. These technologies separate human procreation from the physical act of interpersonal love. To many, this is a violation of God's plan for an intimate union between married love and the children who are the fruit of that love. A technological intervention into the natural rhythms of procreation violates this divinely intended union. What is naturally the most intimate of interpersonal acts is reduced to impersonal procedures and this is against nature.

Secondly, *in vitro* fertilization involves massive abortion of zygotal life. The products of test-tube fertilization are destined for two ends, implantation in a suitable womb (the Baby Louise procedure) and research. Before implantation, artifically produced zygotes are carefully examined for defects. Of course, only completely normal zygotes would be implanted. The rest are destroyed. And most of the normal group don't ultimately survive either, since the procedure is still highly experimental and rarely succeeds. The zygotes destined for research are destroyed after the research is completed. In this country, the general ethical consensus is for a time-frame of three weeks. After this, experiments on developing embryonic life must cease and their growth must not be allowed to continue. Not all countries are so conservative about foetal experimentation. In Swedish laboratories you'll find 22-month-old foetuses, decapitated and wired to scientific monitoring devices.

Thirdly, surrogate motherhood and A.I.D. (surrogate fatherhood) by introducing a third party into the marriage plays havoc with marital fidelity, natural kinship and family bonds. For example, since the identity of male donors is kept anonymous and since one donor makes repeated donations, there is the possibility of incest by children who, unbeknownst to themselves, were produced by the same father. And when a third party enters into procreative union with one of the partners of a marriage, albeit artificially, doesn't this violate the marriage bond?

Fourthly, the spectre of psychological harm has been raised, especially to surrogate mothers and to children of a surrogate parent. The woman who carries a child in her body for nine months only to give it away can be much more traumatized than the male who donates a sperm sample. Further, does the whole climate of this research encourage women to think of themselves as machines of reproduction? Finally, how well can children be protected from finding out about their surrogate parents and how effectively can the emotional impact be cushioned if indeed they do find out?

We pass over here the legal entanglements of all this. The courts have not begun to sort them all out, and until they do the potential for emotional harm is incaculable.

On the other hand, defenders of the new technologies would respond to these objections as follows.

First, scientific intervention into human reproduction is not unnatural (or against God's plan) when science is put at the service of nature. Inability to have a child is a breakdown of the natural reproductive process. Human intelligence, through science, repairs the breakdown, finding ways for nature to produce the babies it could not produce before the defect was circumvented. Test-tube fertilizations and research, the use of surrogate mothers, and A.I.D. are such intelligent circumventions to bring about the intended natural result—new babies, new human life.

Secondly, when zygotal experimentation is carried out under responsible and limited conditions, the gains in knowledge about genetic defects, human conception, and foetal development balance out the termination of zygotal life in these very first two to three weeks after conception. If one adopts an evolutionary view of foetal development (see Question 9—above—on abortion), the goal of increased knowledge could justify experimentation on zygotes; while the same experiments carried out on more mature foetuses would be morally repugnant.

Thirdly, the ethical impact of surrogate motherhood and fatherhood on marital union and family kinship is best understood when compared to adopting a child. In surrogate parenthood, the child carries the genes of one of the two parents who will raise the child. Adoption does not put a wedge into family unity. Even less would the child of a surrogate whose biological kinship is closer than the adopted child's. The issue is not whose egg or whose sperm, but who loves, cares for and nurtures the child.

Also, often much more sacrifice, commitment, and love are required to "make a baby" artificially. Consider, for example, the woman who makes a twice-monthly visit to a clinic for donor insemination, often going for years before the insemination "takes". Is there less interpersonal love shown by her than by the woman who conceives in the act of natural intercourse?

Fourthly, everyone agrees that surrogate procedures must be carried out with great care to guard against the possibility of psychological trauma. Screening for physical health and psychiatric stability is essential both for the surrogates and the couples involved. And everyone must be clear about the safeguards to be taken to protect the sensibilities of the children who result.

ISSUES TO BE RESOLVED. First, are the new conception-technologies an intelligent effort to aid and abet nature to achieve its goals? Or are these unwarranted depersonalized incursions into a reproductive process that should be naturally linked to the interpersonal physical act of married love alone? If the latter, then you will morally reject outright all efforts at artificial conception.

Second, is the zygote, albeit human-like, less than fully human? If so, the search for understanding more about human reproduction may justify experiments on it, experiments that would be repugnant if performed upon a more mature organism. Or is the zygote a fully human person from the moment of conception? If the latter, experimentation as presently practiced will be considered mass murder.

Thirdly, do surrogate mothers and male sperm-donors positively serve the family unity of married couples by helping them have the children they so desperately long for? Or are these third party surrogates and donors to be viewed as intruders who sever the interpersonal bonds of married love? If the latter, then you will see adoption as the only moral recourse for the infertile couple.

Fourthly, as for the potential of psychological harm to surrogates, parents, and their children, there is no disagreement that every precaution should be taken to forestall such harm. There is disagreement about how effectively this can be accomplished in the present cloudy state of the civil laws governing these matters.

AN OPINION. We live in a climate where the Technological Imperative reigns supreme: "Whatever technologically *can* be done, *should* be done". The practice of this principle has given us nerve gas, biological warfare, the hydrogen and neutron bombs. Test-tube fertilization is especially vulnerable to the abuse of the Technological Imperative. In A.I.D. and surrogate motherhood, human life develops in the hiddenness of the womb according to natural biological rhythms. The test-tube zygote, on the other hand, develops out in the open, subject to human intervention at every step of the way. The Technological Imperative puts no restraint on scientists as to how they will tamper with or modify human growth or on what anomalies they will attempt to produce. Dare we trust such Promethean human mastery over the course of human reproduction more than we trust the secret wisdom of biological evolution which is holistically in tune with all of nature? The past results of applying the Technological Imperative don't make one optimistic.

SOME FURTHER READINGS

Anne Taylor Fleming, "New Frontiers in Conception: Medical Breakthroughs and Moral Dilemmas", *The New York Times Magazine* (July 20, 1980), pp. 14ff.

Leon R. Kass, M.D., " 'Making Babies' Revisited", *The Public Interest*, No. 54 (Winter 1979), pp. 32–60.

12.

Why do people worry more about the murderers in death row than about their victims who are already dead?

> Men are not hanged for stealing horses, but that horses may not be stolen.
>
> George Savile, Marquess of Halifax[1]

> Capital punishment has never been and never can be anything but an uncertainty. It is a punishment for revenge and retaliation, not for protection.
>
> Lewis Lawes
> Warden at Sing Sing Prison (1920–24)[2]

THE PROBLEM. Euthanasia is not murder because it is killing with the consent of the killed. Abortion is not murder (say the proponents of abortion) because there is not a fully human life involved. But capital punishment involves an adult human life taken without the consent of the killed. Is this rightly called socially sanctioned murder? Yes, say the opponents of capital punishment. This kind of killing is sheerly vindictive revenge bringing no social good to either the victim or the State. No, it is not murder, say the proponents of capital punishment. The individual by his crime deserves the punishment. And society by the penalty is protected both from this criminal and from future criminals who will be deterred from crime.

ARGUMENTS FOR AND AGAINST. Three reasons are offered for the punishment of criminals. First, punishment is said to help reform the criminal. Second, the order of justice is said to be vindicated or restored: a life for a life, an eye for an eye.

[1]George Seldes (ed.), *The Great Quotations* (Pocket Book edition), p. 800.
[2]Kenneth Jakubowski, "An Evaluation of Capital Punishment" (unpublished ms.), p. 1.

58

This is the vindictive theory of punishment. Third, punishment is said to deter men from crime (the deterrence theory).

Obviously, there is no motive of reform in capital punishment. The capital offender is executed, not rehabilitated. But the social good requires this, say the defenders of the death penalty. Vindictive punishment is not merely selfish and petty revenge wreaked on the criminal. There is an order of justice, an order of reality. Actions have consequences. Excessive drinking brings a hangover; an accident from careless driving brings on a damage suit; money borrowed must be repaid. Society rests on mutual faith that its members will responsibly cooperate with each other. Disorder, if tolerated, breeds more disorder. Carelessness must be atoned for; debts must be paid. When irresponsibility goes without penalty, when debts are not honored, society breaks down.

Capital offenses (treason, murder and, in some states, rape) present the supreme threat to this order of society. Society for its own preservation and morale must close ranks against the capital offender. He has struck at the very roots of society's life. He must die, even if no other potential criminal is deterred by his death. There is an order of justice which must not be mocked. Society's survival rests on men's confidence that this order will be observed. Actions have consequences: a life for a life.

Not only does capital punishment vindicate the order of justice, but it is a necessary deterrent to crime. Why wouldn't the robber kill his victim if he knows that his own life is untouchable? Why shouldn't the fugitive kill the pursuing policeman, or the prisoner his guard? The killer whose own life is securely immune can kill with impunity. Capital punishment is a necessary deterrent to capital crime. Thus the case for capital punishment rests securely on the two pillars of justice and deterrence.

The death penalty's opponents argue that this case, though persuasive as an abstract theory, stumbles on the facts. Capital punishment, far from vindicating the order of justice, is filled with injustices in the way it works. Moreover, there is no evidence that capital punishment is a deterrent to capital crimes.

First, the death penalty works unjustly. It's a poor man's punishment. For example, all of the fifteen men put to death in 1964 were represented by court-appointed attorneys. "They couldn't afford to hire their own," said the warden of the Cook

County jail in Chicago. "If there is enough money behind you, you can usually avoid the chair." The calculated, deliberate murders are those that are committed for hire, and they are backed by the best kind of defense by which convictions can be appealed until execution is eventually avoided.

Nor does capital punishment serve as a deterrent. An effective deterrent depends upon the certainty that it will be imposed. The United States of America averages 11,000 homicidal deaths a year. The annual executions from 1963 till 1966 numbered 21, 15, 7, and 1 respectively. Furthermore, 77% of reported U.S. crimes never get solved. Thus the odds are against getting caught, and once caught the odds are overwhelmingly against getting executed. The man in the death cell more reasonably attributes his fate to a combination of poverty, bad luck and stupidity than to a realization that he is receiving the just punishment of his crime, a punishment which should have deterred him. Moreover, deterrence supposes a rational criminal who calculates all the consequences of his evil deed rationally and coolly. This is a most unlikely criminal—and fortunately so, for rational consideration of the above facts leads to the conclusion that fear of receiving a capital penalty should not deter him from his unlawful act.

Capital punishment has also been defended as mercy killing—i.e., as a fate much more humane than the living death of life imprisonment with no hope of parole. But it is certainly not humane if a mistake was made. There is no redress for the executed victim. If mercy is really the aim, perhaps we should ask the criminal in death row whether he would prefer the mercy of execution to the cruelty of life imprisonment with no possibility of parole. Real mercy would be to rehabilitate the capital offender. He is eminently reformable. In New York State, for example, over a ten-year period, only 7.2% of convicted murderers were convicted of further crimes after being paroled, as compared to 20.3% of the parolees who were guilty of other types of crimes.

ISSUES TO BE RESOLVED. 1. Is capital punishment needed to vindicate the order of justice? Yes, say the proponents. Even at the cost of the individual criminal, society must close ranks against those who attack her vital interests. The assurance of an order of justice in which lethal actions have lethal consequences forms the basis for cooperation and trust among members of a society. Not so, say the opponents. The criminal is the product of society and still a member; he must be reformed, not excluded. Society is strengthened when her sick members are restored, not when they are cut off.

2. Is capital punishment needed as a deterrent to crime? Yes, say the proponents. If the desperate man is assured that his life is immune, nothing will stop him from killing. No, say the opponents. Deterrence doesn't work. The criminal does not calculate the consequences of his crime, and even if he did he would conclude from the facts that the punishment is unlikely to follow the crime.

AN OPINION. It is possible that deterrence would work if society would expend greater efforts to achieve swift, sure, impartial and universal justice. But society is recently coming to see more clearly that the deviant is part of her makeup and not to be cut off as an alien thing. As long as the leper was treated as an outcast from society, no progress was made against leprosy. As long as the mentally ill person was caged and confined from ordinary society as an inhuman and alien thing, no progress was made against mental illness. As with leprosy and mental illness, so with crime. The fruitful approach seems to lie in looking toward its conditions and causes. Until society dared to see its own disorders mirrored in her fellow-human lepers and mentally ill, she excluded them as a race apart, thus perpetuating her ill and theirs. Can we dare see the mirror of our own disorder in the criminal and face the pain of restoring him to ourselves?

SOME FURTHER READINGS

Michael DiSalle, *The Power of Life or Death* (New York: Random House, 1965).

Edward McGhee and William Hildebrand, *The Death Penalty* (Boston: D. C. Heath and Co., 1964).

PART IV
Marriage and Sexuality

13.

Is marriage too personal to be defined?

> Matrimony is always a vice; all that can be done is to excuse it and to sanctify it; therefore it was made a religious sacrament.
>
> St. Jerome[1]

> Marry such women as seem good to you, two, three, or four, but if you fear you will not be equitable, then only one.
>
> The Koran[2]

THE PROBLEM. There are as many views of human sexuality and marriage as there are societies, and sometimes it seems that there are as many views as there are people. In moral questions regarding human sexual behavior we follow the same principle we have been using all along: "nature is the measure of action." If we can discern the dimensions of human sexuality and marriage—i.e., what its nature is—then we will have a framework in which to judge how to act accordingly in the questions of divorce, trial marriage, homosexuality and birth control. As a framework for these questions we will here consider two views of sexuality most common in the United States: (a) the view, espoused by Bertrand Russell in its most extreme form, that sexual behavior is solely the concern of the consenting adults involved, and anything they decide is morally permissible provided that no one is harmed; (b) the view that sexual behavior has many more dimensions than the purely private decision of the parties involved: there are biological, psychological, interpersonal and social dimensions that cannot morally be ignored. Let it be noted that in this chapter we are concerned with the morality of only the mar-

[1]*The Great Quotations*, op. cit., p. 643.
[2]*Ibid*, p. 644.

ital-genital exercise of sexuality, while readily conceding that sexuality pervades every aspect of human living.

TWO VIEWS OF SEXUALITY. The purely private view of sex rests on a philosophy which stresses human individuality and freedom. It presumes that we are talking about adults, not children. As an adult I am free and responsible for my freedom—and I am alone in my freedom. I cannot evade this responsibility by letting my actions be dictated by an outside force, be it a Church, or society, or a conventional moral code. This would be to surrender to another the central core of my person, namely, my free responsibility for shaping my own life. As in my whole moral life, so in my sexual behavior: what I do rests on my responsibility alone. There is only one qualification. If I freely choose to enter into a sexual relationship with another, I must respect his or her freedom too. I must not harm the other. For consenting adults, any freely agreed upon sexual relationship is morally good provided that no one is harmed.

Such free and responsible love and respect is the only norm. Granting this norm, it makes no difference whether the relationship is heterosexual or homosexual, marital or extramarital, permanent or casual, loving or purely physical. Marriage, in Russell's view, is a moral and legal necessity only when children are involved. Lest the children be harmed, the parents must enter upon the legal partnership of marriage to ensure the stable home and education which children need.

In what we will call the holistic view of sex, there is more involved in sexual behavior than the purely private decision of the parties involved. Sexual behavior has biological, psychological and social ramifications as well as individual aspects. To act without consideration for these wider aspects of sexuality is to be irrational and immoral, for it would be action done in blindness to the human realities involved. What is the full human reality of sexuality in what we call the holistic view?

A first look at sexuality reveals the fundamental but not terribly startling fact that the human race is divided into males and females in roughly equal numbers. This biological fact is obvious, but not without ethical significance. Do we have a first hint here about the adequacy, the rationality and the morality of homosexuality as an ideal?

Second, in addition to the biological dimension of human sexuality, there is the social dimension which is equally fundamental and unmistakable. The sexual faculties are procreative. They are oriented toward the continuity and development of the human species. This is not to conclude that they must always be used procreatively. But it would be more than naive to deny that they have anything to do with procreation, or to claim, for example, that sexuality is a purely private affair. The survival of the race is inextricably involved with the exercise of sexual intercourse.

What has been said so far is true of both human and sub-human animals. But in the human, the biological and procreative aspects of sexuality are at the service of the whole person: sex is personal and interpersonal. My growth as a human person is intimately bound up with my sexual relationships. Do we get some light here as to the adequacy and morality of depersonalized sex, or sex without love and commitment, even permanent commitment?

Finally, there is the individual dimension of sexuality. This is the insight emphasized in Russell's view. My growth in freedom and responsibility as an individual is a function of my sexual behavior. I am not subordinate to the race. My individuality is constituted by my free and responsible control of biological sexuality functioning in a social context as an expression of and fostering interpersonal love. Do we have a hint here about the adequacy of any morality which would make procreation the primary and overriding purpose of marriage?

TWO VIEWS OF MARRIAGE. These two opposing views of sexuality result in two opposing views of the nature of marriage. For Russell, marriage is purely a legal arrangement between a man and a woman who are going to have children. Its only purpose is to avoid harm to the children by providing them with the stability needed for their nurture and education. Marriage concerns procreation only. If there are no children and no harm done, then sexual behavior may morally take any form chosen by the parties involved.

In the holistic view, sexuality is a much less arbitrary and more complex phenomenon. It has an individual dimension: the free and responsible use of sex in terms of all the human realities involved. Part of this human reality is the biological dimension: it is a relationship between a man and a woman, not between a man and a man, or a woman and a woman, or an individual with himself. This biological dimension exists in a personal context. Sex between a man and a woman is an expression of personal love and commitment; complete sexual surrender is a sign of total and permanent commitment. This personal commitment exists in society (the social dimension) with the possibility of children as the fruit of their love contributing to the growth of society. The name of this complex relationship is marriage. In this view, genital-marital is a hyphenated word. Biological, social, interpersonal and individual are intimately interrelated. The human reality of sex involved in these interrelationships discloses that genital sex is a function of marriage. Marriage is the free and complete commitment of a man and a woman to each other, expressed by interpersonal procreative love, and witnessed publicly by the society to whose continuation and growth they contribute.

AN OPINION. The holistic view of marriage presents in outline form the philosophical rationale behind the Judaeo-Christian concept of marriage in Western civilized society. There have been varying emphases even within this tradition. For example, in the past Roman Christianity emphasized the biological and the procreative to the detriment of the personal and individual. In such an emphasis, interpersonal and psychological values take second place to procreative values in judgments about such things as birth control.

The holistic view of sex stands or falls by how closely you see all the dimensions to be intertwined. Obviously they *can* be separated. For example, physical sex can take place without personal commitment. The basic question is this: Does such separation tend to foster or to destroy the complex human realities of human sexuality?

SOME FURTHER READINGS

Sidney Callahan, *Beyond Birth Control: Christian Experience of Sex* (N.Y.C.: Sheed and Ward, 1968).

Edward Ford, *Why Marriage?* (Niles: Argus Communication, 1974).

Philip Keane, S.S., *Sexual Morality: A Catholic Perspective* (Paramus: Paulist Press, 1977).

Mary Perkins Ryan, *Love and Sexuality* (Garden City: Doubleday and Co., 1969).

14.

Is divorce ever intelligent and moral?

> Getting divorced just because you don't love a man is almost as silly as getting married just because you do.
>
> Zsa Zsa Gabor[1]

> When I can no longer bear to think of the victims of broken homes, I begin to think of the victims of intact ones.
>
> Peter De Vries[2]

THE PROBLEM. Marriage is understood in the Western world as, in some sense at least, a permanent union. The marriage vows end with the words "until death do us part." Presumably, though the partners may separate, neither may marry another as long as either one lives. The commitment was "until death." How seriously are these words to be taken? How permanent is permanent? Should the marriage formula be re-worded? Would it be more honest to strike out the words "until death do us part" and substitute "until we are bored" or "until we are broke" or "until either of us commits adultery" or "until either of us becomes seriously ill?"

ARGUMENTS FOR AND AGAINST. Your view of divorce is the reverse side of the coin of your view of marriage. The basic question is this: Does divorce with remarriage square with the realities of human sexuality, especially the personal commitment implied? Obviously, in Russell's view of marriage there is little difficulty. Marriage is solely an arrangement to prevent harm to children. If divorce and remarriage would prevent greater harm, then this is the only intelligent and moral thing to do. But what about the holistic view of marriage and sexuality? Can

[1]Barbara Rowes, *The Book of Quotes* (N.Y.C.: Ballantine Books, 1979), p. 99.
[2]*Ibid.*, p. 95.

divorce ever be squared with the complex human reality presented by this view? A utilitarian case can be made for divorce and remarriage in extreme circumstances. A personalistic case can be made against it.

As in the case of war, so also in divorce; no one is for it. At best, it is at times a necessary evil. At times the consequences of divorce and remarriage seem less harmful than the consequences of continuing an impossible union or separation without remarriage. These situations should be relatively rare, though the statistics of actual divorces compared to the number of marriages do not seem to bear this out. Divorce is a major upheaval in the life of the partners and at best an emotional trauma for the children. The only possible utilitarian justification for such an upheaval and trauma is in order to avoid an even greater upheaval and trauma.

One need not have lived very long to be able to think of such extreme cases. Think, for example, of a young girl, married at sixteen, who has three quick children and then is abandoned by a philandering husband at the age of nineteen. Suppose this older and wiser woman now has the possibility of marrying a more stable and mature man. Her children would have a father and she would have the chance to rebuild a life for herself on the ruins of her first marriage. Which is the greater evil: to live out her days alone, her children without a father, because of her fidelity to a man who abandoned her and whom she will never see again, or to try to make a new home for herself and her children by a divorce and remarriage?

This is not an argument for easy divorce. The temptation should be avoided to argue from such extreme cases to the conclusion that divorce is the solution to most marital difficulties. A bad dancer doesn't become a better one just by changing partners. Indeed, a utilitarian case can be made out against easy divorce. Consider the following figures and ask yourself what is the state of the human reality of marriage in the United States today. On one side of the ledger, write down 3,000,000 marriages per year. On the other side, write down 800,000 divorces plus 1,000,000 separations, plus 100,000 desertions, plus 13,000,000 children now growing up in broken homes. This is hardly an argument for divorce as a panacea.

Easy divorce goes hand in hand with easy marriage. While

a utilitarian case can be made out for divorce in extreme cases as a last resort, a personalistic view sees marriage as a definitive, personal, total life commitment involving my goal and identity as a person. The resulting union, therefore, cannot be broken, since I have staked my life and moral worth upon my fidelity to this commitment. The marriage consent is not a utilitarian affair where I rationally calculate the consequences and give my consent "provided everything works out as I foresee it." That is why the marriage formula is worded "until death," and not "until this or that disillusionment occurs." When two people stake their whole identity as humans on their life together, they are promising more than they can possibly know. There is great risk, and illusions will be shattered at every step of the way. Hopefully, on the foundation of these shattered illusions there will emerge growth in freedom and strength and maturity as persons—in a word, growth in the ability to give and love.

How many people realize or even intend to make such a complete and serious commitment? Very few, if we look at the divorce statistics. What about the extreme case of the abandoned young mother of three children mentioned above? Probably there was no such definitive and total commitment. Probably the parties were even incapable of it. A divorce here wouldn't really be a divorce, but a recognition that no marriage had taken place. In this view, a total commitment either is or it isn't. If there really was a mutual total gift and commitment to each other, then it's done. There can be no sense in talking about undoing it. That would mean it wasn't total to begin with. There *is* sense in saying that it wasn't total to begin with. This is not divorce, but a statement that no marriage ever took place. Such is the personalistic case against divorce.

ISSUES TO BE RESOLVED. 1. Is marriage a purely legal agreement to live together as long as we can attain certain foreseen benefits and certain disillusionments don't take place? If this is marriage, then divorce becomes simply a matter of weighing consequences, and choosing the less evil set of consequences.

2. Or is marriage a total, mutual, personal commitment in which we stake our moral worth on our life together, our children, and whatever unforeseen challenges the future may hold, with the hope of growing in freedom, maturity and love? If this

is marriage, then divorce is impossible. "Divorce" in the sense of recognizing that such a firm commitment never took place would be possible.

AN OPINION. There is no divorce problem in the United States. There is a marriage problem. If easy marriages are allowed, it would be intolerable not to have easy divorce laws. Should easy marriages be allowed? That depends on your view of what marriage is. If the personalistic view reflects the human realities involved in sexuality and marriage, then it is foolhardy and immoral to take marriage lightly. If marriage is a purely legal arrangement for pragmatically foreseen goals, then there is no moral obstacle to easy marriage laws. The social evil of 13,000,000 children now living in broken homes would make one wonder whether this is the more realistic view of the human realities involved in marital sexuality.

SOME FURTHER READINGS

Charles E. Curran, *Ongoing Revision in Moral Theology op. cit.*
Stephen Joseph Kelleher, *Divorce and Remarriage for Catholics* (New York: Doubleday, 1973).
Lawrence G. Wren, *Divorce and Remarriage in the Catholic Church* (New York: Newman Press, 1973).

15.

What is to be said about "trial" marriages and other informal living arrangements?

> Marriage is a friendship recognized by the police.
> Robert Louis Stevenson[1]

> Marriage is a book of which the first chapter is written in poetry and the remaining chapters in prose.
> Beverly Nichols[2]

> Sex is so casual and taken for granted. I mean, we go to dinner, we go home, get undressed like old married people, you know—and just go to bed. I mean, I'm not saying I'd like to be raped on the living room floor exactly. But I would love to just sit around on the sofa and neck.
> Hunter College student[3]

THE PROBLEM. Divorce raises the question of whether the marriage consent involves permanent commitment. Trial marriage raises the question of whether the human reality of sexual intercourse involves permanent commitment. We use "trial marriage" as an umbrella term to include intimate living arrangements entered upon without legal sanction by church or state. Trial marriage has been proposed as one solution to the marriage problem discussed in the previous question of divorce. Is this solution feasible? "Yes," some argue. "Commitment is a gradually growing thing. It does not happen at the magic moment of the marriage ceremony. Premarital intercourse, with love and re-

[1] From Leonard Louis Levinson, *The Left-Handed Dictionary* (N.Y.C.: Collier Books, 1966), p. 138.
[2] *Ibid.,* p. 139.
[3] Norman Vincent Peale, *Sin, Sex and Self-Control* (Fawcett Crest reprint, 1967), p. 56.

sponsibility, as long as no harm is done, is part of this growing commitment."

To this line of reasoning, others retort: "This new sexual morality is an illusion. Extramarital sexual intercourse always causes harm because it involves in its very reality the kind of personal commitment which can only take place in marriage. It is a sign of total giving. But the only gift is marriage. It promises more than it gives. Therefore, it can't help but be destructive."

ARGUMENTS FOR AND AGAINST. First, whatever is to be said about premarital intercourse, there is no question but that the commitment of two people to each other is a gradually evolving thing. That's what engagement is all about. It is unrealistic to expect, and it is hopefully not the case, that at one minute before the wedding ceremony the man and woman are a detached and disinterested couple with perhaps a platonic friendship, whereas at one minute after the wedding ceremony they are totally committed to each other, body, mind and spirit until death. On the other hand, is it really true to say that there is no difference at all in the commitment of of the engaged couple before the ceremony and the commitment of the married couple after the ceremony? Commitment is a growing thing. But *almost total* commitment is one thing, *total* commitment is another. In other words, is there a difference between being married and being "all but married"?

This distinction can get blurred. Regular and planned intercourse without a feeling of love and often without some kind of commitment to marriage is rare. But if couples are engaged, it is felt to be definitely allowable. Often the process is reversed. When sexual intimacy has reached the point where decision has to be made about engaging in intercourse, this serves as a pressure to direct the relationship toward marriage. "Love makes it right so long as nobody gets hurt." Intercourse thus practiced with responsibility and respect is felt to solidify the relationship. Sexual compatibility is tested, and the couple learns to integrate this dimension of their lives into their other goals and responsibilities. This expression of love is felt to be all the more urgent in view of the long engagements often necessitated by prolonged graduate studies, military service and the impossibility of immediate marriage. Intercourse saves a meaningful relationship from withering and dying away. No harm is done to anybody. Interpersonal growth is the norm.

On the other hand, is it really true that nobody gets hurt? The permissive position is flawless if engagement is the same as marriage. But engagements, even long engagements, *are* broken. In such cases, by no means rare, would not the woman especially feel "used"? Does this very real possibility indicate that sexual intercourse without permanent commitment is perhaps irresponsible? Furthermore, their bodies are expressing total giving, but their lives are still separate. Such an intimate practice of love often is a moral pressure for two people to marry before they are really free and ready to do so. Is this intelligent or responsible?

There is further evidence that permissiveness in practice is not as beautiful as it sounds in theory. The Kinsey report found that women who had had premarital sex were twice as likely to be unfaithful after marriage than those who did not. This throws some doubt on "trial" marriage as the best preparation for marriage. Further evidence concerns pregnancy and V.D. It is alleged, and it seems reasonable, that drugs and contraceptives have eliminated these two fears which used to inhibit premarital intercourse. But the rate of extramarital pregnancies has increased and V.D. is soaring. This seems unreasonable, but it's not too surprising. The sexual impulse is the very life force of the species. When it is given full expression in regular sexual intercourse, it does not readily heed the demands of reason. This is another reason why it has been the experience of mankind that total sexual expression demands stable family structure: in our culture, the total commitment of monogamous marriage. The evidence points to the human reality that sexual intercourse is a total bodily giving which irresistibly implies a total personal commitment—which is another name for marriage, and engagement is not marriage.

ISSUES TO BE RESOLVED. 1. Which is the true story about engagement? (a) We are married in our hearts; we don't need a wedding ceremony to tell us we are married. (b) When people are really married in their hearts, what's to prevent them from making it public in a ceremony; if they are not ready to get married the second way, it is doubtful that they are married the first way.

2. Which is the true story about intercourse without the to-

tal commitment of marriage? (a) It need not harm anybody; it fosters personal growth and maturity, and is a good preparation for married commitment. (b) It is irresponsible; it is a total bodily giving which does not reflect life commitment; damage can come both from broken engagement as well as from premature marriage formed either by pregnancy (increasingly common in spite of contraceptives) or by the psychological pressure brought on by such sexual intimacy.

AN OPINION. In the area of sexual behavior like no other, the immediacy of the good blots out the realization of possible long-range harm. Mere negative sexual prohibitions are totally ineffective. But great hope for intelligence and morality lies in the stress on personal, loving responsibility in one's sexual relationships. Responsible love will not seek immediate good at the price of the real possibility of long-range harm. We have focused on sexual intercourse because even in the New Morality this intimacy is linked with some orientation to marriage. Responsibility in lesser intimacies can be judged by their relationship to commitment and eventually to marriage.

Of course this whole discussion has no point if the reader accepts Russell's view of sexuality discussed in the last two questions. Our discussion has proceeded on the assumption that sex is more than a purely private interaction like playing tennis or dining out. Our argument has assumed that sex has profound effects for good or ill on both the persons involved and on society.

SOME FURTHER READINGS

Evelyn Millis Duvall, *Why Wait Till Marriage?* (New York: Association Press, 1965).

Richard McCormick, S. J., "Notes on Moral Theology: Pre-Marital Relationships", *Theological Studies* (March 1973), 77–92.

Norman Vincent Peale, *Sin, Sex, and Self-Control* (Fawcett Crest reprint, 1967).

16.

Is homosexuality a moral question?

> Homosexuality is assuredly no advantage, but it is
> nothing to be ashamed of, no vice, no degradation, it
> cannot be classified as an illness. We consider it to be
> a variation of the sexual function, produced by a cer-
> tain arrest of sexual development.
>
> Sigmund Freud[1]

> Wherefore just as in speculative matters the most
> grievous and shameful error is about things the
> knowledge of which is naturally bestowed upon man,
> so in matters of action it is most grave and shameful
> to act against things as determined by nature. There-
> fore since by the unnatural vices man transgresses
> that which has been determined by nature with re-
> gard to the use of venereal actions, it follows that in
> this matter this sin is the gravest of all.
>
> Thomas Aquinas[2]

THE PROBLEM. Thought—or, better perhaps, strong feeling—
about homosexuality runs the whole gamut from uncompromising moral denunciation to the view that it is a perfectly accept-
able variant on human sexual behavior. We confine our concern
here mainly to overt homosexual behavior and ask whether it is
sin, or illness, or a variation on normality. As our consideration
of premarital sex threw some light on the personal commitment
involved in sexuality, and our consideration of divorce threw
some light on the permanency of that commitment, so hopefully

[1]From a letter written in 1935, quoted by Henri J. M. Nouwen, "Homosexuality:
Prejudice or Mental Illness?" *National Catholic Reporter* (November 29, 1967),
p. 8.
[2]*Summa Theologiae*, II, 154, 12 and 4.

the consideration of homosexuality will throw some light on the bi-sexual dimension of human sexuality.

We will focus on the male homosexual defined as "one who, apparently physically normal, is entirely unsusceptible to the sexual and emotional attraction of the opposite sex, but is susceptible to the sexual and emotional attraction of his own sex." Between 2% to 4% of the male population fall under this definition, which does not include bi-sexuals or homosexual behavior due to circumstances (e.g., as occurs in prison or in cases of youthful experimentation). We will look at homosexuality from a medical and a moral perspective. The purpose is not so much to provide moral guidelines for the homosexual, but rather to help clarify the attitude of the non-homosexual population toward him.

PERSPECTIVES ON HOMOSEXUALITY. A first view, common among homosexuals, is that there is no problem about homosexuality. The problem is one of prejudice toward the homosexual. Polymorphous sexuality rather than heterosexuality characterizes the human animal. In a culture which puts a premium on heterosexuality, the homosexual is defined as deviant and immoral. But there is nothing that says that sexual love cannot be directed toward members of one's own sex as well as toward the opposite sex. The loneliness, immaturity and defensiveness of homosexuals are normal reactions to the prejudice of others rather than a symptom of emotional illness or moral turpitude. This, you will recall, is completely in line with Russell's philosophy of human sexuality.

The holistic view of sex challenges this view that heterosexuality is purely a culturally defined ideal. Biologically, there are two sexes. Their attraction and complementarity are common to all cultures. Their sexual cooperation is essential to the survival of the species. In a biological framework, heterosexuality is more than an accident of culture. Not as unequivocal, but nevertheless strong, is the evidence that psychological and personal growth is a function of heterosexual rather than homosexual relationships which tend to be unchallenging, impermanent and static. In a word, sex viewed in its whole human reality is a heterosexual affair. If this is the way it is, then homosexuality cannot be held up as a moral ideal.

Does this mean that the homosexual is inherently immoral?

No. It is a defect in maturity rather than a failure in morality. There is a psychiatric view, increasingly under challenge, that homosexuality represents an arrest in sexual development. Whereas most children, after a stage of homosexual attraction, pass on to interest in the opposite sex, the homosexual for emotional and environmental (but not physiological) reasons does not move on to heterosexual interest but remains fixated at the earlier stage. He is no more morally responsible for this disturbed emotional pattern than other people are for their other types of neurotic emotional patterns.

Granting that the homosexual is not morally responsible for his feelings, is he morally responsible for overt homosexual acts? Moral responsibility is proportioned to the freedom and self-awareness with which an act is done. Both of these qualities are impaired, but not necessarily removed altogether, in actions which flow from neurotic emotional patterns. Take the case of a heterosexual adult, who has normally strong sexual drives but who for some reason is not married and may not marry, and who in some facets of his sexual life is emotionally immature. How responsible is such a person for his overt heterosexual acts? The answer would be the same for the homosexual. No special moral condemnations are in order.

ISSUES TO BE RESOLVED. 1. Is human sexuality basically heterosexual or is it polymorphous? In other words, is heterosexuality a cultural accident or is it basic to the human sexual animal? Or is homosexuality an equally valid expression of human sexuality?

2. Is the homosexual morally responsible for his sexual orientation, or is this orientation the product of sexual fixation due to the emotional environment in which he was raised?

3. Is the homosexual fully responsible for his overt homosexual acts, or is he no more or less responsible than would be a disturbed unmarried heterosexual for his overt heterosexual acts?

AN OPINION. Since lesbianism is surrounded with less legal and cultural prejudice, it was not part of our treatment here. Doubtless many of the homosexual's problems are directly traceable to such prejudice rather than to his sexual disorder. A comparison of male and female in this area might shed light on the factor of prejudice. The human being with homosexual orientation is first of all a human being, not a homosexual.

SOME FURTHER READINGS

David Loovis, *Straight Answers About Homosexuality for Straight Readers* (New York: Barnes and Noble, 1978).
Letha Scanzoni and Virginia Ramey Mollenkott, *Is the Homosexual My Neighbor?: Another Christian View* (New York: Harper and Row, 1980).

17.

Does birth control violate the natural law?

> Equally to be excluded, as the teaching authority of the Church has frequently declared, is direct sterilization, whether permanent or temporary, whether of the man or of the woman. Similarly excluded is every act, which either in anticipation of the conjugal act or in its accomplishment, or in the development of its natural consequences, proposes, whether as an end or as a means, to render procreation impossible. . . . Man cannot find true happiness . . . other than in respect of the laws written by God in his very nature, laws which he must observe with intelligence and love.
>
> Pope Paul VI[1]

> Likewise, we take exception to some of the specific ethical conclusions contained in the encyclical. They are based on an inadequate concept of natural law. The multiple forms of natural law theory are ignored, and the fact that competent philosophers come to different conclusions on this very question is disregarded.
>
> Reply to Pope Paul VI[2]

THE PROBLEMS. A lot of water has gone under the bridge in the past few decades concerning the birth control question in Roman Catholic circles. These vicissitudes have not been without impact on the wider political and legal scene. Narrower sectarian questions concerning teaching authority and doctrinal development have been raised for Catholic theologians. We confine

---

[1]Pope Paul VI, Encyclical *Humanae Vitae,* July 25, 1968.
[2]Quoted from the dissenting statement of Roman Catholic theologians to the Encyclical *Humanae Vitae,* July 30, 1968.

ourselves here, as we have throughout the book, to the philosophical issues involved. From this point of view, the Catholic fight reflects a transition from a cyclic Greek view of nature and natural law to a more experimental and evolutionary view of nature and moral law. As we asked in Part I, is nature a book for humans to read, or for humans to write?

A further problem concerns the term "birth control," which covers everything from complete abstinence from sexual intercourse to abortion. An objective natural law approach might accept abstention as a method of birth control while rejecting the use of anovulant pills. Similarly, the evolutionary approach might accept the use of anovulant pills while rejecting abortion as a method of birth control. While the purpose—namely, birth control—is the same in all these cases, the methods used raise special moral issues of their own.

ARGUMENTS FOR AND AGAINST. 1. *The Methods of Birth Control.* There is not space here for anything like an adequate description or discussion of the following methods. The purpose of this listing is simply to suggest in outline form the kind of moral issues to be considered when coming to a decision as to which, if any, method to use. The listing is in order of contraceptive effectiveness, with the figure in parentheses representing the pregnancy rate in terms of number of children per hundred women per year: 1. complete abstention from intercourse (zero); 2. tubal ligation (1.6); 3. oral hormone pill (some maintain that the rate for users of "the pill" is zero if it is taken properly); 4. the IUD: intrauterine device (2.4); 5. condom (14); 6. diaphragm (14); 7. rhythm (approximately 25–35); 8. douche (41); 9. no method (80); 10. a so-called "morning after" pill to be taken after intercourse and designed to prevent the fertilized egg from implanting itself in the womb. Constant experimentation is developing other methods: pills with smaller quantities of hormones to lessen bad side effects, subcutaneous hormonal implants, vaccines, and contraceptive drugs for males.

Methods 2 and 3 involve sterilization, permanent and temporary; the moral issue is whether a contraceptive intention can justify the permanent or temporary inhibition of a bodily function. Methods 5, 6 and 8 intervene in the act of intercourse itself, preventing the sperm and ovum from joining: the moral issue is whether a contraceptive intention justifies the prevention of the act of intercourse from effecting what it would effect (a fertilization) if there were no intervention. Methods 1 and 7 involve permanent or temporary abstention from intercourse; the moral issue is whether the very intention of contraception is moral or not in the marital relationship, one dimension of which, as we have seen, involves procreation. Methods 10 and 4, according to some *inconclusive* evidence, involve the aborting of the zygote in the very first days after conception; the moral issue is whether a contraceptive intention justifies the termination of this immature and undeveloped foetal life. More evidence is needed to determine just how the IUD works.

In summary, the methods of birth control raise the moral issues of: (1) contraceptive intention (all the methods, including rhythm and abortion); (2) sterilization or intervention in a bodily function (tubal ligation and the anovulant pill); (3) intervention preventing an act of intercourse from effecting what it would otherwise effect (condom, diaphragm, douche); (4) abortion of a fertilized ovum before it is implanted in the uterus ("morning after" pill and perhaps the IUD).

2. *Two Approaches to These Issues.* In medieval natural law ethics, nature was viewed as a book in which the moral law might be read. Nature might not, therefore, be "tampered with." Although this position has been softened in order to allow the kind of tampering which goes under the name of science, a line was drawn to the extension of science to the control of the sources of human life—i.e., to the control of procreation or birth control. Medicine and fertility studies are permissible, inasmuch as they foster nature. But scientific efforts to prevent the procreative faculties from having their natural effect is an immoral tampering with nature.

Even this latter position has been softened to allow for the use of rhythm and abstention in married life. Rhythm and abstention may have a contraceptive intention. A married couple may morally intend that the procreative activity not result in procreation if they have a good reason for such birth control. To achieve this contraceptive intention, they may, by the practice of periodic abstinence, limit sexual intercourse to the days in the menstrual cycle when the woman is infertile. Even though their intention is that their procreative faculties do not achieve their natural end which is to procreate, this is morally allowed since they are not *doing* anything to frustrate the function or the act. They are refraining from doing—i.e., they are abstaining from intercourse.

Some natural law ethicians have further softened their position to allow for temporary sterilization by the use of the anovulant pill. Since the contraceptive intention can be morally licit, nature's own hormones can be used to achieve their natural effect—i.e., the prevention of ovulation. The act of intercourse still proceeds unimpeded. Even nature herself allows periods of infertility in the female. The anovulant pill is only using nature's way to extend this infertile period when there is a legitimate contraceptive intention. The act of sexual intercourse itself is not tampered with.

The other approach to this question views nature in an evolutionary and scientific context as a book which man writes in a responsible way. There is complete agreement with the softened natural law position that there are occasions when there is reason to limit procreation. Intelligent morality demands that parenthood be undertaken in a responsible fashion. Responsible reasons for limiting procreation can range from the purely individual (another pregnancy would endanger the life of the mother) to the nationwide (in Chile 30,000 children die annually before the age of one, 20,000 of these from hunger). If the intention is responsible and good, then responsibility also demands that the means used be as effective as possible. For example, where responsible intelligence calls for contraception, it would be irresponsible, other things being equal, to use rhythm rather than some more effective method if it were available, be it an anovulant pill or a mechanical device. Responsible morality demands that man bring nature, including his own procreative nature, under his intelligent control. In this view, then, granting a good reason for contraception, any method short of abortion would be morally good. What about an abortifacient agent like the "morning after" pill? This would depend on the position you take on the abortion question as the issues were drawn up in the previous chapter.

ISSUES TO BE RESOLVED. 1. Is nature a book to be read and followed blindly or a book to be written with intelligence and responsibility?

2. If the former, does a contraceptive intention (that the procreative faculties do not procreate) violate nature, or may one negatively, by practice of periodic abstention, attempt to achieve a contraceptive end, if one does not positively do anything to interfere with nature?

3. In the same framework, does the use of anovulant pills assist nature in nature's way, or is it a tampering with nature and hence immoral?

4. On the other hand, if nature is a book to be intelligently and responsibly written by human beings, is every method of birth control open to moral consideration, or are abortifacient agents like the "morning after" pill ruled out of consideration?

AN OPINION. The moral issues have been lined up in terms of opposing views of nature and natural law, where the birth control question has cut the deepest. Today, even within the Roman Catholic Church, there has been a movement away from rigid natural law ethics, but past teachings made in this framework remain to be explained. Today perhaps, in Roman circles, it is the theological problem of teaching authority and development of doctrine that cuts the deepest.

Concerning each of the methods of birth control there are subsidiary factors which must be weighed in coming to an intelligent moral judgment. We cannot ignore the bad physiological side effects of hormonal pills or the psychological difficulties which arise in connection with the use of rhythm or of mechanical devices. Another point, not emphasized in our treatment, is the sincerity and honesty needed in evaluating the reason for birth control. One might, for example, question the wealthy hedonistic couple's concern for India's starving millions as a reason why they themselves never want to have any children. As we have seen, marriage in the holistic view is a complex multifaceted reality of which procreation is one dimension, a dimension linked with the social, interpersonal and individual dimensions bound up in every marriage. How children are to be integrated into the rich human reality which is their marriage is every couple's responsible decision.

SOME FURTHER READINGS

Pope Paul VI, Encyclical *Humanae Vitae.*

Statement of Roman Catholic theologians dissenting from the aforementioned Encyclical (printed in *The New York Times,* July 30, 1968).

John T. Noonan, *Contraception* (Mentor-Omega paperbound, 1965). This is a definitive history of the practice and attitudes toward birth control throughout the history of mankind to the present.

Margaret Nofziger, *A Cooperative Method of Natural Birth Control* (Summertown, TN: The Book Publishing Co., 1976).

Barbara Seaman and Gideon Seaman, M.D., *Women and the Crisis in Sex Hormones* (Bantam Books, 1977).

PART V
Social Justice

18.

What does society owe to the individual member? Does everyone have the right to a guaranteed annual income, to open housing and integrated schooling?

> The only ones benefitting from the way they're running things now are bums, deadbeats, and people who just don't give a darn about earning a living.
>
> A Massachusetts garage owner[1]

> It's been a struggle for me because I had a chance to be white and I refused.
>
> Richard Pryor[2]

> To be a revolutionary you have to be a human being. You have to care about people who have no power.
>
> Jane Fonda[3]

THE PROBLEM. Human society is unimaginable without discrimination. Not to discriminate among humans would be unrealistic, unintelligent and immoral. Discrimination rests on two incontrovertible facts: (1) human beings are not equal; (2) human beings are different from one another. Discrimination is a recognition of these inequalities and differences so that one's conduct may be guided accordingly.

On the other hand, it is true to say that "all human beings are equal" and that "all human beings are not different: they share a common humanity." To discriminate among them as if some were superhuman, some human and some sub-human would be unrealistic, unintelligent and immoral. Refusal to dis-

---

[1] Quoted in *America* (November 26, 1966), p. 680.
[2] Rowes, *op. cit.*, p. 117.
[3] *Ibid.*, p. 57.

criminate here is the recognition of the common humanity that one person shares with others so that one's conduct may be guided accordingly.

Failure to discriminate where discrimination is due is called injustice. Suppose I have two applicants for the job of store detective, one a compulsive kleptomaniac and the other a former police officer retired in good standing. Other things being equal, it would be unjust of me to hire the compulsive thief in preference to the experienced officer. Here, discrimination is clearly just.

Discrimination can also be unjust. Suppose a teacher has two pupils who perform exactly the same on an arithmetic test; one pupil has a cute freckle-faced brown-eyed smile, the other does not; she gives the former a higher grade because he reminds her of her own son. Here, refusal to discriminate would be just. The discrimination was clearly unjust.

Therefore, discrimination is sometimes just, and discrimination is sometimes unjust. This moral issue of discrimination is splitting American society today, especially in the following three areas:

1. Poverty discriminates, putting the poor in a class apart; welfare regulations are an attempt to discriminate between the deserving and the undeserving poor; guaranteed annual income is a proposal which refuses to discriminate among the poor. Here, which is just and which is unjust—discrimination or refusal to discriminate?

2. Protected neighborhoods are an attempt to discriminate between racially desirable and racially undesirable neighbors; open housing is a proposal which refuses to discriminate among those economically able to join the neighborhood. Here, which is just and which is unjust—discrimination or refusal to discriminate?

3. Neighborhood schools are an attempt to discriminate between who should be educated together on the basis of place of residence; busing is a proposal which refuses to accept the residency requirement as a basis for school attendance. Here, which is just and which is unjust—discrimination or refusal to discriminate?

Note, too, that even the non-discrimination proposals above involve discriminations on other levels. Guaranteed annual income does discriminate between rich and poor. Open housing in some of its forms does discriminate between those who can afford to buy or rent a house and those who cannot. The moral issue is not simply whether discrimination is good or bad. The whole problem is that it is sometimes just and sometimes unjust. This chapter will discuss first the morality of discrimination, and then indicate some of the moral issues involved in deciding the justice or injustice of guaranteed annual income, open housing and integrated schooling. Our concern is not with specific income or housing or schooling proposals but with the moral issue of discrimination which lies behind the acceptance or rejection of such proposals.

ARGUMENTS FOR AND AGAINST. 1. *The Case for Discrimination.* The case for discrimination in the area of poverty and race relations does not rest on any intention of degrading the poor or of reducing those of another race to sub-human status. While loving them as fellow human beings, the discriminator wants at the same time to face unsentimentally the realistic fact of differences and inequalities. I would like to have a summer home on the seashore, says the discriminator, but my salary is not large enough. You don't find me complaining that I have a right to a summer home. It is a fact of life that some people have more money than others. This is a difference we have to live with. We make economic discriminations in every area of life. Some people you are willing to risk lending money to, others not. This is economic discrimination of a very intelligent and necessary kind. Therefore, when the poor want money handed out to them, I am not being inhuman when I say no. I'd like money handed out to me too. But I don't demand it as a right because I recognize the fact that people are different in what they own and what they can earn, and that money doesn't grow on trees. Discrimination between the rich and the poor is just and necessary. Anything else is naive sentimentality.

Not only is economic discrimination a necessary fact of life, unpalatable as it may be for people like myself who would like to have more money, argues the discriminator, but discrimination in whom I choose to associate with is a necessary and important fact of life. I like to go bowling with the guys from the factory. I would not be comfortable bowling with the gals from

St. Agatha's Church. And I'd be very surprised if they started claiming that they had a right to bowl with me, that they had a right not to be discriminated against. Rather, a man does have a right to discriminate among the people with whom he chooses to live and work and play and those he does not. I have no intention of degrading the women's bowling group as sub-human. I respect them as fellow human beings. I just don't want to bowl with them. And I respect the right of the Friendly Sons of St. Patrick not to welcome me, an Italian, into their group. Not only are people economically unequal, but they are different in a thousand other ways. Discrimination is simply the recognition of this fact. This is why we have different clubs, different customs, different leagues—yes, and different neighborhoods and different schools. The goal of wiping out the differences among people, or of pretending that they don't exist, is an unrealistic pipe-dream, and even very undesirable. To say that someone is different, and that I therefore prefer not to live with that person or join his or her club, is not to say I don't love and respect him or her as a fellow human being. Such people may well be better than I am. I just prefer to live with my own kind.

Not only are people unequal in wealth and different as to whom they'd rather associate with, but how people dispose of their property is a matter of their own choice and discrimination. Suppose I owned a high-precision camera that my German-born neighbor really liked and wanted to buy from me. Then suppose I went and sold it to my cousin instead. I'd be very surprised if my neighbor began demonstrating against me for not selling to him, and for discriminating against Germans. After all, it was my camera. I can use it as I please when I own it, and dispose of it as I please. A person has a right to discriminate in the use and disposal of property. That's what it means to own something. And the fact that I discriminate in favor of my family, my friends or my nationality doesn't mean that I look on others as less than human. I just prefer dealing with and helping my own kind.

As a matter of fact, the discriminator's argument continues, in my book all persons are fellow humans. You don't hear me shouting for rights for this group or that race or this or that nationality. These are the people who are labeling humans and pitting one group against another. These are the divisive people in society. If a person is human, he or she is my friend. I wouldn't insult such a person with a racial or economic label. For all our differences we are all basically human. We should act that way, and not split ourselves up into groups demanding special treatment.

2. *The Case against Discrimination.* The case against discrimination in the area of poverty and race relations does not rest on the naive refusal to recognize that people are unequal and different, any more than the case for discrimination implies that those discriminated against are sub-human. It is granted that people are economically unequal. Everyone does not have the right to own a yacht. It is granted that people are socially different. Every man does not have the right to belong to the Friendly Sons of St. Patrick. It is granted that people have the right to discriminate in the choice of how they dispose of their property. Everyone cannot claim an equal right to buy the pure-bred dog I want to sell. The fact that I can't own a yacht does not make me less than human. The fact that I am ineligible for the Friendly Sons or unable to buy your dog does not make me less than human. Discrimination is just and good when it recognizes the differences among people, and when these differences do not imply that I am less than human.

On the other hand, discrimination is unjust when it makes the differences among people the basis for treating some in a human way and others in a less than human way. Here is the point at issue in the argument for and against discrimination. Am I being discriminated against as a *human being?* This is unjust. Every human has the right to be treated as a human being. It is unintelligent and immoral not to treat human beings for what they are. Am I being discriminated against as a particular *kind* of person? This is just, provided that I am being treated with dignity and respect as a *human being.* I have a right as a human not to be left to starve to death. Discrimination which means starvation is unjust. It is not a right but a privilege to belong to the Friendly Sons of St. Patrick. Discrimination which makes me ineligible does not violate my rights as a human being. Is welfare or a guaranteed annual income a right I can claim as a human being or a privilege which society may or may not grant me as it pleases? Is buying the house I can afford my right as a human being (open housing) or a privilege (protected neighborhoods)? Is integrated schooling my right as a human being (busing) or a

privilege (neighborhood schools)? How do I tell rights from privileges? How do I distinguish unjust discrimination from just?

The advocates of welfare and guaranteed income, open housing and integrated schooling claim these as rights, not privileges.
The non-white and the poor live in American society, fight for
American society in disproportionate numbers and contribute
cheap labor to American society, thereby enabling others to live
disproportionately well. But the non-white and the poor do not
share in the benefits of the American society in which they live
and for which they fight and to which they contribute. Discrimination which prevents people from getting out of the society
what they contribute is unjust. This is why the poor and non-
white feel that they are being treated as less than human.
Through no fault of their own they are refused participation in
society and relegated to its fringes. This is not a harmless discrimination among acquaintances, but a discrimination on the
part of the majority of society which is snuffing out the human
light in millions of fellow human citizens. It is not enough to *say*
that I respect you as a human being when by my votes and *actions* I ensure that your high infant mortality rate will continue
and your children will be assured an inferior education and
hence a life without equal opportunity. This is not discrimination
among humans but inhuman discrimination, and it is a matter
not of words but of facts.

Poverty is no respecter of races. But nonetheless blacks fall
below the poverty line as compared to whites by a factor of more
than three. Infant mortality, too, is three times as high. So is un-
employment. And the same goes for their share of income and
their share of technical and professional jobs.

It may be granted that hot running water, a well-balanced
diet and a low mortality rate are not necessarily connected with
being human. Indeed, in the year 100 A.D. and even later, there
were contented, intelligent, loving, hope-filled human beings
who had no running hot water or balanced diets or low infant
mortality. But a man's self-respect, dignity, hope and ability to
develop are a function of his ability to participate in, function in
and be accepted by the society in which he lives and finds his
identity. The conditions for hope-filled human development in
America in 1981 are different from the conditions for hope-filled
human development in Polynesia in 1281. I can live with hope

if my society accepts me, needs me and lets me share in its work and growth and play. To the dead-end poor in America today, society is saying: "I don't need your help; I don't want to live with you; you are a burden on me; I wish you would go away." This is the human significance of running hot water, medical care, job opportunities and adequate sanitation. It's the difference between saying "You're a fellow human and I want you to be part of me" and "You're less than human; stay apart from me where you belong." Few people discriminate so bluntly in their words. It is actions, backed up by dollars-and-cents priorities, which freeze the poor out of the ongoing society at large. This is discrimination with a punch to it much more effective than words.

In line with this argument, the advocates of welfare and of a guaranteed annual income view each as a human right of the poor, not an arbitrary privilege. My identity, dignity and self-respect as a human being depend on my ability to live and share in that society of which I am a part. This is what it *means* to be human. No man is an island. Being human is something you *are*. It is not something you have to *earn*. An estimated 97% of welfare recipients are either aged or disabled or mothers with small children. They cannot hold full-time jobs. Does this mean they are not to be human beings. Are only full-time wage earners to be regarded as human in the eyes of society? Are the rest subhuman? This is what we saw above as unjust discrimination: discrimination which treats a person not merely as different or unequal but as less than human.

The present welfare system grudgingly admits that even non-wage earners shouldn't starve. At least this much human dignity is recognized. But the complex bureaucracy necessitated by the complex category system under which welfare benefits are administered is degrading and demoralizing to the recipient. It imposes restrictions which encourage continued dependency on welfare—and half of the poor are excluded completely. These limitations have led to greater acceptance of the idea of guaranteed income as a substitute for welfare, preferable even on sheerly pragmatic grounds. Guaranteed income accepts the moral premise of welfare (namely, that economic discrimination is antihuman) and extends a basic human income to *all* the poor.

Guaranteed income, by eliminating most of the need for bureaucracy, proposes to be much cheaper to administer. It would provide an incentive to work by not reducing payments by one dollar for every dollar earned. It would eliminate the degrading personal checkups, searches and inquiries into family life that are part and parcel of the present welfare system. And it would cover all of the nation's poor, not just a little more than the half who are covered now. Many of the poor under this system would become more productive and self-sufficient. And most important-ly, the millions of children, not covered now, will have a better chance of escaping from poverty, a better chance of participation in their own society—a better chance, in a word, of being treated and accepted as humans.

Thus, on the one hand, we have seen the position of the dis-criminator who regards the division between rich and poor as a fact of life to be faced but not to be worried about. There always have been and always will be rich and poor. I can accept the fact of poverty, let the poor stay poor and still love them as human beings. Against this it is argued that this is unjust discrimina-tion. The poor do not have the conditions for a life of human dig-nity, self-respect and growth; the facts show that this is the inevitable consequence of grinding poverty. I cannot claim to love the poor as human beings when by vote and action I contin-ue to ensure that they lead sub-human lives.

Our treatment here is, of course, mainly concerned with drawing up the moral issues involved in our response to poverty rather than weighing the merits or demerits of specific proposals of a guaranteed income. What we have done is to examine whether the poor have a moral right to some kind of aid (what-ever be the specific proposal) or whether such aid is your moral privilege to give or withhold as you please. Your answer depends on whether, in your view, poverty involves sub-human living, or whether it is consistent with a hope-filled, intelligent, loving de-velopment as a human being.

4. *The Inhuman Results of Racial Discrimination.* Let us briefly look at two points where a similar issue is raised in the area of race relations in America today: open housing and inte-grated schooling. Is buying the house I can afford my right as a human being (open housing) or a privilege ("protected" neighbor-hoods which exclude black residents)? Your answer will depend on whether or not exclusion from a neighborhood because of race involves rejection as a human being. Is integrated schooling my

right as a human being (to be brought about if necessary by busing or by some other method such as school pairing, open enrollment or boundary changes) or is it a privilege (that goes with living in a particular neighborhood, for example)? Your answer will depend on whether keeping non-resident blacks out of white schools involves their rejection as human beings.

We have already seen above the argument on the side of just discrimination. A person's property is his or her own. Ownership precisely means the power to discriminate as to how I want to use or dispose of my property. When I refuse to sell my house to a member of another race, I am not rejecting that person as a human being. I am simply using my right as an owner to discriminate in favor of my family or friends or members of my own race. Therefore, open housing is not a moral obligation.

The same argument is used for just discrimination with regard to those with whom I associate. To be in favor of neighborhood schools is not to reject non-residents as human beings. It is simply to say that I prefer my children to be in school together with their friends and neighbors. People are different. That's why there are different clubs, societies and leagues. To face these differences and to prefer to associate with my own kind is not to reject the others as sub-human. Therefore, integrated schooling is not a moral obligation.

In answer to these positions it is argued that to exclude someone from housing because of race is to reject that person as sub-human, and to exclude a non-resident child from a school because of race is to reject that child as sub-human. Again, as in the case of poverty, this rejection is not a matter of words. The words and intentions may be completely sincere, but this rejection is a matter of *fact*. This rejection is equivalent to excluding the man or child from ordinary participation in the life of the society to which he belongs and to which he contributes. It is equivalent to saying: "You don't belong to us; you are worthless; we don't accept you as a full and free participant." It condemns the man and the child to live in the sub-human environment we spoke of in connection with poverty. I can be refused membership in the Friendly Sons of St. Patrick without losing the conditions for hope-filled human growth, but to refuse free and integrated living and education is to cut one out of the basic, human, social life of a society. It is to cut one off as a man.

The facts of black housing and schooling confirm that this is the case. Separate is not equal in housing now. Blacks are second-class citizens, second-class humans as a matter of *fact*. Separate is not equal in education now. Blacks are second-class citizens and second-class humans as a matter of *fact*. Worse still, the continuation of this kind of discrimination ensures a growing alienation of blacks from the society of which they are a part— a growing dehumanization of blacks, in other words.

Separate is not equal in housing now. Nationwide, 25% of all non-whites live in central cities in substandard units compared to 8% of all whites. Moreover, blacks pay the same and receive less. Blacks in housing means segregating them as humans. Separate housing means unequal human living. Unequal human living means unequal human beings.

The problem is not only with housing. Separate is not equal in education now. In the critical verbal skills and reading ability blacks fall further behind whites with each year completed. Behind 1.6 grades in the sixth grade, they are 3.3 grades behind white students in the twelfth grade.

Worst of all, this pattern of discrimination, if not reversed, promises a growing alienation and dehumanization for blacks. Future jobs are being created in the suburbs, but the chronically unemployed are increasingly concentrated in the ghettos. Housing outside the central cities is essential both for learning about job opportunities and for travel to work. Racial and social-class integration is the most effective way to improve the education of ghetto children, as well as to remedy the naiveté of even more racially isolated white children regarding poverty and segregation. Moreover, to give the mass of blacks true freedom of choice as regards housing, there will have to be incentives for new construction of low- and middle-income housing and an uncompromising policy of open housing. These measures to heal the rifts of de facto racial segregation are directed toward the survival of our society as one society, which is another way of saying our survival as human beings. Ostracism from the group on which he depends is the worst penalty a society can inflict on a member. Solitary confinement in prisons leads to madness. Discrimination because of race which leads to permanent inferior education and housing, and hence to permanent, ostracism from the work and benefits of the society on which the black must depend, is a form of solitary confinement; for this reason, it is a type of discrimination which is anti-human. Certain kinds of discrimination can be just and moral, but anti-human discrimination is certainly unjust and immoral. In addition, racial discrimination regarding education and housing as practiced in American society is anti-human. This, in brief, is the moral argument against discrimination in matters of race.

ISSUES TO BE RESOLVED. Discrimination which respects humans but recognizes realistically their differences and inequalities is just and moral; discrimination which is anti-human, which as a matter of *fact* (whatever be the words or good intentions) relegates those discriminated against to a less than human life, is immoral and unjust. Three problem areas of discrimination were raised in this chapter: (1) the discrimination involved with poverty versus welfare, and welfare with its discriminating category system versus guaranteed annual income for all alike; (2) protected housing which discriminates against racially "undesirable" neighbors versus open housing for all alike; (3) neighborhood schools which result in de facto segregation versus integrated schooling for all alike. The issue in each case is similar. I must ask myself whether the discrimination involved in each case results, as a matter of factual evidence, in a life that is less than human for those discriminated against. If so, this particular type of discrimination is immoral. If not, then this particular type of discrimination is harmless and moral. The question is not whether I feel benevolent toward those who are discriminated against. The question is what the actual results of the discrimination are, regardless of my benevolent feelings. The point of this chapter is not the merits of a particular guaranteed income program or a particular busing program or a particular open housing law. The point is the morality of the discrimination which such programs are trying to remedy. It is readily granted that a particular proposal may involve more harm than good. The point raised here concerns the moral reason for having such proposals at all.

AN OPINION. The main point of this chapter was to raise the question of whether racial discrimination is a relatively harmless quirk, or essentially anti-human. The problems touched on only scratch the surface. Behind all of the problems lies the problem of the pervasive, destructive, dehumanizing force of segregation. A child who depends for his life on his family but is not allowed to know any of the family secrets or to share in the family projects or to contribute in any way to the life of the family or to live with the rest of the family will soon be a very sick child. Segregation has caused such sickness in American society. In the view of this author, black separation is a counsel of despair. It may be a measure that is temporarily necessary to achieve the identity and self-respect denied by the larger society, but jobs and progress and integration with the national and world community lie with the larger society. Separate will mean unequal and inferior.

A final observation concerns the nature of prejudice. Its touchstone is not lack of love, but lack of justice. Every northern boss prides himself on greeting his black janitor by his first name and exchanging pleasantries with him. Blacks have always been loved "in their place." It is a question not of love, but of justice. De facto segregation de facto dehumanizes, and it calls for some de facto measures which will shatter the rules of the game. Proposals like busing and guaranteed income shatter the rules of the game. The white man who loves the black and wants to keep all the ground rules as they are now in all probability is at least unconsciously prejudiced. This judgment is based on the view of this writer that the ground rules, as they are now, are anti-human for blacks.

SOME FURTHER READINGS

John Arthur and William Shan, *Justice and Economic Distribution* (Englewood-Cliffs, N.J.: Prentice-Hall, Inc., 1978).

Daniel C. Maguire, *A New American Justice: Ending the White Male Monopolies* (Garden City: Doubleday, 1980).

Thomas Nagel, "Equal Treatment and Compensatory Discrimination," *Philosophy and Public Affairs* (Summer 1973), 348–363.

19.

Is gender-difference relevant to the fair treatment of human beings?

> Human beings are not animals, and I do not want to see sex and sexual differences treated as casually and amorally as dogs and other beasts treat them. I believe this could happen under ERA.
>
> Ronald Reagan[1]

> The emotional, sexual and psychological stereotyping of females begins when the doctor says, "It's a girl".
>
> Shirley Chisholm[2]

THE PROBLEM. Women and men, precisely as human, are equal, and in justice are owed equal treatment as human. A sexual caste system which would relegate one sex to an inferior human status, and grant the other a superior status, would be immoral and unjust.

Women and men, precisely as biologically different, deserve in justice, it would seem, to have these biological differences respected. While maintaining equal treatment as human, does biological distinction imply *equal but different* treatment on the basis of sex?

If gender distinction is a relevant basis for different treatment, what form should this treatment take? When does "different" become "unequal"?

These questions involve male and female alike. We approach them from a feminist angle because this is where the best thinking has been done.

ARGUMENTS PRO AND CON. Consider three current models of womanhood: (1) The Traditional Woman: "Woman as Wife and

[1]Rowes, *op. cit.*, p. 33.
[2]*Ibid.*, p. 28.

Companion"; (2) Moderate Feminism: "Woman as Person linked in mutual self-interest with Man as Person"; (3) Radical Feminism: "Woman as Person (Oppressed) at war with Man as Person (Oppressor)".

The model of woman as Wife and Companion emerged in the 1920's. It was a stroke of liberation. It moved woman from life centered on the nursery to become man's equal companion at home and in the bedroom. Rejected was a life centered exclusively on children and on companionship with other women. Rejected was a life, segregated from men, nursemaid to children and activist with the suffragettes and the Woman's Christian Temperance Union. Wife-companion became free to pursue her own personal interests, within the home and as ruler of the home and free to enjoy her sexuality. She felt equal to or superior to males, not discriminated against but privileged. Margaret Sanger and the birth control movement legitimated this new freedom; alimony and divorce laws gave it social support.

As female, Traditional Woman is complement of the male. Her definition is the reciprocal of his. She is helpmate, companion, lover; his masculine qualities are complemented by her feminine ones.

Restrictions on self-expression were cast aside. Women could smoke, dance with abandon, raise their hemlines, and bob their hair. The romantic ideal of marriage was born. The young woman's main curriculum centered on finding the "right man". Charm schools sprang up everywhere.

The agenda of Traditional Woman today is to preserve family and woman's role in the family. It is to safeguard from feminist erosion the legal structures that give plausibility to her role; alimony, support laws, and exemption from the military protect her privileged position as female, complementary and equal to the male, but still different. For the Traditional Woman, "biology is destiny".

The Moderate Feminist refuses to define woman by reference to man. She is not his "better half". She is a whole Person linked with man as a whole Person. Her respect for herself as a person liberates him, too, from role-bound definitions; together they can be genuine partners pursuing autonomously their independent paths.

The Feminist rejects confinement to a life centered on the

home, the garden, the suburbs, the cub scouts, the volunteer services. She does not feel bound to become caterer for her husband's business associates; nor is she obsessed with supporting his ego or tiptoeing around after his "hard day at the office."

As human beings, woman and man are equal in every way. Workplace practice, social custom, and many laws violate this human equality. The feminist is bound to do away with these. She wants no "privileges" from the law protecting her "femininity". Give her her human rights; she'll take care of her own privileges. She is proud of being a woman, but biology is no impediment to her making the same life choices that any man can make.

A wave of new legislation and revision of many social institutions reflects this view of Woman as Person (rather than Wife-Companion). Consider Equal Rights legislation in many states, the Supreme Court's abortion decision, Title VII of the Civil Rights Act, the Equal Credit Opportunity Act, the establishment of Child Care Centers, the acceptance of pregnancy leaves for both males and females. Society is saying, This is an OK way to be. Woman as Person becomes more and more plausible as the credibility structures for Wife-Companion gradually crumble away. The Feminist tells Wife-Companion that she is benefiting too. But it's harder and harder to insist credibly that a woman's place is in the home with the emergence of so many legal and social gateways leading out of the home.

But Woman as Person still needs all the plausibility structures she can get. Barriers of attitude if not of law still stand in the way of her exercising her self-chosen life-options. But Woman as Person will without apology compete with males, compete with other women, participate in all sports, enter all professions, do any job that a male does, study any field.

Feminism's main agenda is to make Woman as Person the national norm of Womanhood by legitimating it in the U.S. Constitution itself by passage of the Equal Rights Amendment. And aside from this, the major thrust is for equality in the workplace, pushing into the wings less central issues like lesbian rights or even free day-care centers.

Radical Feminism is another story entirely. Woman is a human Oppressed, indeed massacred, by Man the Oppressor. She forms a systematically Oppressed class. The Moderate Feminist view of Woman as Person linked with Man as Person is ridiculously optimistic. Women and men are not engaged in a win-win game. There's a war on, there always has been. It's a zero-sum game. There are winners and losers, and until now women have been the losers.

Radical Feminism rejects the Moderate's agenda centered on breaking into male-dominated institutions. The Radical especially rejects the alliances with men necessarily and naively entered upon in the pursuit of this agenda. You don't do business with the enemy. Within present institutional structures, looking for job access, equal salary structure, access to clubs, equal credit opportunity, changes in marriage laws, access to church ministry is all a dead end. It is buying into the male game where another way will be found to subdue and reduce you to your subservient place. In some ways this turn in the Feminist Movement had its counterpart in the racial movement. "Black Power" replaced the vision of "Blacks and Whites together" marching toward human equality. In Radical Feminism, the Women's Movement takes a similar turn.

Under the pretense of treating women as different but equal, men have defined women as different and inferior, and have developed social institutions to lock them into a sub-human caste. Men are the movers and shakers, exercising the reason and will that make human beings *different* from the other animals. Women bear the burden of reproduction; one half the human race bears this burden for the whole. Women are reduced to this function which the human *shares* with the other animals. As humans, women are locked out of equality with men.

The legitimation of this outrage is the weight placed on gender-distinction. To the Radical Feminist, it is preposterous to divide the human race according to genitals. Gender-distinction is as irrelevant to humanness as color of hair and color of eyes. The centrality of humanness and the irrelevance of gender is expressed by Ti-Grace Atkinson by using the generic term "Men" to refer to human beings. There are men who inseminate, and there are men who get pregnant. And all men have the right to freedom in these matters. And all men share equally in the burden of responsibility for the kids who turn up on the scene. It's not "role of mother", "role of father", etc.; it's a matter of two people who have kids, and what are we going to do about them. The options are completely open on the economic issues, the child-rearing issues, the "family structure" issues. Gender has nothing to do with it. But preposterously, this is not now the way it is; gender has become a stigma for enslavement of "females".

Plausibility structures for a gender-free world have still to be created. Our present laws, social customs and institutions make gender central to being human. We think that this is the way it has to be. We find it hard to imagine a world of persons with irrelevant gender differences, a world without Mr., Mrs., Ms., or Miss; a world without gender-related magazines, shops, living arrangements, clothes. The first step toward such a world is the agenda of the Radical Feminist. It is to expose the political rape that has robbed half the human race of their humanity by making them the reproductive beasts of burden for the whole.

ISSUES TO BE RESOLVED. The validity of the Wife-Companion Model as compared to the Woman as Person Model revolves around one major issue. A recent statement by the Catholic Bishop of Newark exemplifies it. "Women," he said, "should assume their equal but different roles alongside of men in the Church." Are women equal but different as human beings? Or are they equal as human beings, period? Is there gender-based input into the meaning of human? If so, it is the human right of women to have their differences respected, and when necessary, to have the privileges of their sex enshrined in the law. Such is the view of the Traditional Woman. If not, then women have the human right to be treated equally and the same as men. Discrimination on the basis of sex becomes unjust. This is the view of the Feminist.

Neither Moderate nor Radical Feminist defines Woman by reference to the male. She is a complete Person in her own right. The issue between them turns on Woman's relationship to Man. Is he partner or enemy? If partner, then the liberation of Woman will at once be the liberation of Man, both freed to pursue autonomous role-free lives as whole persons. If enemy, then the liberation of Woman involves the defeat of Man in his present entrenched position as Oppressor. Her gain can occur only at the price of his loss.

AN OPINION. Each model has its problems when it attempts to impose a single definition on women of all times and places. Traditional Woman is a middle class model. The poor have always had to work outside the home. They've never been able to enjoy the domestic "privileges of their sex". Out in the male workplace they desperately need the protections and rights that the Feminist would have them enjoy.

Moderate Feminism is a First World phenomenon. This becomes evident at every International Women's Conference. The plight of women in less developed cultures involves much more radical surgery than envisioned by their more affluent sisters. The rhetoric of class oppression comes easily to the forefront. But even granting the pervasive (economic especially) discrimination against women in America, is the radical critique entirely applicable here?

SOME FURTHER READINGS

Midge Decter, *The New Chastity and Other Arguments against Women's Liberation* (New York: Coward, McCann and Geoghegan, Inc., 1972).

Germaine Greer, *The Female Eunuch* (New York: McGraw-Hill Book Co., 1971).

Mary Briddy Mahowald, *Philosophy of Woman: Classical to Current Concepts* (Indianapolis: Hackett Publishing Co., 1978).

Sheila M. Rothman, *Woman's Proper Place: A History of Changing Ideals and Practices, 1870 to the Present* (New York: Basic Books, Inc., 1978).

20.

Global justice: Are we aboard lifeboats or a spaceship?

The North-South debate is often described as if the rich were being asked to make sacrifices in response to the demands of the poor. We reject this view. The world is now a fragile and interlocking system, whether for its people, its ecology or its resources. Many individual societies have settled their inner conflicts by accommodation, to protect the weak and to promote the principles of justice, becoming stronger as a result. The world too can become stronger by becoming a just and humane society. If it fails in this, it will move towards its own destruction.

Commission on International Development[1]

People vary. Confronted with appeals to limit breeding, some people will undoubtedly respond to the plea more than others. Those who have more children will produce a larger fraction of the next generation than those with more susceptible consciences. The difference will be accentuated, generation by generation.... To make such an appeal is to set up a selective system that works toward the elimination of conscience from the race.

Garrett Hardin[2]

THE PROBLEM. In 1974 and 1975 the United Nations General Assembly called for a "New International Economic Order" (NIEO). It drew up a program for redistributing power and

---

[1]North-South: A Program for Survival—Report of the Independent Commission on International Development Issues (Cambridge: M.I.T. Press, 1980), p. 33.
[2]Garrett Hardin, *Exploring New Ethics for Survival* (New York: Viking Press, 1972), pp. 258–259.

wealth and for reorganizing global economic institutions. This NIEO is designed to redress the vast disparities that exist between the more affluent nations of the northern hemisphere, on the one hand, and the LDC's of the southern, where over-population, hunger and poverty abound.

At stake is the basic question of distributive justice: Who gets what and why? There have emerged toward this global problem of distributive justice two contrasting responses, popularly labelled Lifeboat Ethics and Spaceship Ethics. Garrett Hardin, advocate of the former, condemns efforts to aid fatally weak nations as a misguided idealism that will only make matters worse for poor and rich alike. Daniel Callahan, chief respondent to Hardin, sees human travellers as morally bound to each other on a single global spaceship. Which is the truer picture of the world? Which morality is more responsive to our meaning and worth as human beings? We'll examine each model in turn.

ARGUMENTS PRO AND CON. According to Hardin, the world is best conceived as a group of lifeboats. The rich-nation lifeboats are well-appointed and have ample room for their passengers. Poor-nation lifeboats, on the other hand, are overflowing. These passengers, pushed overboard, are thrashing about in the water, hoping to get aboard the rich boats and grab a share of the "goodies" that the wealthy passengers enjoy. What should the rich lifeboats do?

The people in the rich nations are self-sufficient, surviving well by controlling their resources and birth-rate. If they let the hordes of irresponsibly multiplying poor on board to plunder everything they have, rich lifeboats and poor alike will go under.

Some misguided idealists see the globe as a single spaceship on which rich and poor alike are fellow-passengers sharing a common goal and common resources. Who is the captain of this ship? There is none. Who is allocating the common resources? Who is controlling the growth of population? No one. The spaceship is a model for cooperation. This is an illusion. There is no hand at the tiller; there is no common goal. The reality is not cooperation, but competition by independent nations to maximize their share of a limited pie. The Lifeboat is a survival model calling for a survival ethics.

So protectionism, not generosity, is the rule of the day. Generous aid to the over-breeding poor nations will only encourage further over-breeding and over-consumption, hastening the day of disaster for all.

This is a *consequentialist* ethics. Charity is justified by results. When charity brings disaster, charity is counterindicated. A survival ethics calls for the *triage* approach used by doctors in time of disaster. The *triage* approach gives results. Divide the survivors into three groups, those who can help themselves, those who are fatally wounded, and those who can be helped to help themselves. The first group can be trusted to survive on their own. The second should be written off and allowed to die, so as to concentrate all efforts on the third who with help will survive. In this way we should divide the nations of the world. Hopelessly poor and over-populated nations should be allowed to go under. True mercy here is mercy-killing, benign neglect, passive euthanasia.

How tell which nations are survivable and which fatally ill? A nation which cannot or will not take determined and effective population control measures is a candidate for euthanasia. Population control has to be an absolute pre-condition for aid. The alternative is the "tragedy of the commons". Two farmers graze five cows each on a common field sufficient to graze ten. Farmer Jones slips in a sixth cow. The other ten cows have a little less grass, but Jones has a whole extra cow. He has no self-interested motive to show restraint. Farmer Smith then adds a cow, and the process goes on till all the cows grow skinny and die. Such is the tragedy of the commons. Irresponsible nations keep adding people to the detriment of all nations, especially of those which show restraint. In the situation of the commons, restraint is self-defeating. That's why when you agree to split the lunch bill, it's to your interest to order the most expensive item on the menu. So population control must be a pre-condition for aid: no more than five cows, a $4.00 ceiling on the entree. Nations who won't do this must be let die, lest all die.

Daniel Callahan sharply challenges Hardin's Lifeboat ethics. Nations are not like isolated lifeboats. Rather, we are global passengers on a single ship. The upper deck (the northern hemisphere) is the commercial and recreational center. It obtains supplies, resources, and fuel from below deck (the southern hemisphere). The passengers are interdependent. The cutthroat model of competing lifeboats is an illusion. The reality is the co-operative interdependency imaged by the Spaceship model. True, there is no captain, i.e., no world government; but economic bonds bind more tightly than political. First-world lifestyle would crumble without Third-World imports and markets. To act on the assumption of a false self-sufficiency is a prescription for disaster.

What is called for, then, is not protectionism but a generosity based both on self-interest and justice. The *consequentialist* ethic of Hardin falls short in matters of justice. Callahan's approach is *deontological:* human beings are ends in themselves. Never should a human being or a group of human beings be written off or sacrificed for the welfare of other human beings. The genocidal prescriptions of the *triage* approach are morally repellent. The hungry, starving poor are just as deserving of life and food and human dignity as the well-fed and affluent.

Hardin's "tragedy of the commons" tells a distorted tale of what's really going on. We can increase our common resources in two ways. First we can develop them more ingeniously, evolving better sources of energy and improving agricultural techniques. Secondly, we can eliminate wasteful consumption, especially as conspicuously and extravagantly practiced by affluent nations.

And Hardin has the matter of population control completely backwards. Experience shows that population control is a *consequence* of socio-economic gains, not a *pre-condition* for them. Babies are the social security and life insurance of the poor. When people sense their lives to be more secure, they reduce their birth-rates. Effective population control must come from below, not from above. It is irresponsible in the extreme to advocate genocide by benign neglect as the price of a nation's not implementing dubiously effective population programs. Protect and support the weak and they will become strong and control themselves, and we will all be the stronger for it.

ISSUES TO BE RESOLVED. Which image paints the more accurate picture of the relations among nations today? Do we live in a world of insufficient lifeboats where some people must be left to drown lest everybody sink? Or do we live on a Spaceship where weak and strong passengers alike depend on each other, and it is in the best interests of the strong to help the weak?

Is moral good to be judged by *consequences,* the greater good for the greater number of people? If so, we might justify the *triage* approach, sacrificing the weak so that the strong majority might live and live well. Or is justice a matter of duty *(deontological)* demanding that every human life has its own dignity which may never be written off or sacrificed for the good of someone else?

Must population control be a *pre-condition* of aid, lest we be overtaken by "the tragedy of the commons"? Or is population control the *consequence* of socio-economic wellbeing? In other words, will unconditional aid to over-populated nations increase the problem or alleviate it?

AN OPINION. It is dangerous to argue ethical issues by metaphor. Metaphors have an attractive simplicity. They give people a sense of having grasped the whole picture. But the reality is much more complex. The metaphor can be a useful heuristic device to sharpen understanding of one or more aspects of that reality.

Hardin's lifeboats sharply point out that our resources aren't limitless. And they force us to take a hard look at the human right to procreation and at possible limits to that right. The wholehearted adoption of the Lifeboat metaphor, however, can seduce us into adopting with it also the "last resort" *triage* solution when we are not yet in a "last resort" situation.

Callahan's spaceship rightly encourages us to be concerned with every passenger, however weak. Our destinies are intertwined. The metaphor, however, can seduce us into buying overly-idealistic solutions. Cooperation aboard ship is a must. But we cannot close our eyes to mutinies and threats of mutinies— mutinies that could dump us into Lifeboats!

SOME FURTHER READINGS

Daniel Callahan, "Life-Boat Ethics", *The Hastings Report* (December 1974).

Garrett Hardin, *Exploring New Ethics for Survival* (New York: Viking, 1972).

James B. McGinnis, *Bread and Justice: Toward a New International Economic Order* (Ramsey: Paulist Press, 1979).

Postscript

The attempt to cover in so brief a space so many and such vast issues is quite ambitious. The purpose will have been served if readers are stimulated to bring some thought of their own to bear on these complex issues—if only to object and refute in their own minds the bias which shows through this writer's presentation of the issues. As a friend of mine with an uncertain command of the English language used to quaintly put it: "There are pros and cons on both sides of the argument." He was usually more right than he knew.